Praise for *Why Bother?*

"Here is what I know about Jennife. _____ force for good in this world. Her life force is off the charts— girlfriend is *alive*. She does not bypass sorrow or rage but meets them fully and turns them into joy. She has single-handedly created a life of unique meaning, authenticity, and abundance that also happens to benefit countless others. If anyone ever asked, 'Hey, want to read a book about how to be just like Jen Louden?' I'd say, 'HELL YES.' And now here it is. This powerful, real, funny, wise book will show you how to stop tormenting yourself with self-doubt and start living your one true life—not by becoming someone else, but by finally being exactly who you are."

SUSAN PIVER, author of *The Four Noble Truths of Love*

"In *Why Bother?* Jennifer Louden shows with great honesty that feeling what is ours to feel is how we endure our way into a more authentic dream where who we are is more than enough. Without being prescriptive, this book is a strong and sensitive companion on the path of becoming fully human. It will help you unravel your entanglements and live."

MARK NEPO, author of *Drinking from the River of Light* and *The Book of Awakening*

"I ended my own book with the words, 'Now what?' When I picked up Jennifer Louden's book, I felt as if it were a follow-up to my own question. *Why Bother?* spoke to me as if I were speaking to myself (in a loving voice, instead of the jerky one) and it has become my guide, my map, my bible, my confidante. I want everyone I know to own a copy as tattered as mine."

JENNIFER PASTILOFF, author of *On Being Human*

"A truly brilliant book. Jennifer Louden is warm, down to earth, and thoroughly practical as she explores the profound question of what matters most to each of us. It's quite stunning how she weaves together personal stories, deep reflections, inspiration, and immediately useful actions. A gem."

RICK HANSON, PhD, author of *Resilient: How to Grow an Unshakable Core of Calm, Strength, and Happiness*

"This book is a revelation. *Why Bother?* woke me up from my creative slumber and revitalized the desire I had pushed to the side in favor of 'getting things done.' Jennifer Louden's words gave language to the areas of my life that felt stagnant, and immediately catapulted me into the action my soul craved. If you've been looking to tap back into your truest desires and deepest purpose so you can craft a life of meaning, this book will help you do exactly that."

AMBER RAE, author of *Choose Wonder over Worry: Move beyond Fear and Doubt to Unlock Your Potential*

"I love this book like I love my closest girlfriends because just like them, it is funny and smart and brave. Like them, it is comfortable with the mess and the vulnerability—in me and in life. Like them, it digs into the details, the nuances of how we forge our paths, the stuff it often seems no one is willing to talk about. Whenever I put it down, I craved going back to it for more mentorship and comfort. It's a truism among us personal-growth writers that everything we are writing about has been written about a thousand times before, but I'm telling you—this book has never been written before."

TARA MOHR, author of *Playing Big: Practical Wisdom for Women Who Want to Speak Up, Create, and Lead*

"*Why Bother?* is for cynics and optimists alike. It's a brilliant map from despair to devotion, and the story of a woman's path home to herself. Jennifer Louden has created an honest account of what it truly means to question everything during our most painful times and emerge powerful and clear, without a self-help cliché in sight."

SUSAN HYATT, author of *Bare: A 7-Week Program to Transform Your Body, Get More Energy, Feel Amazing, and Become the Bravest, Most Unstoppable Version of You*

"I have never felt so seen reading a book. Jennifer Louden is the coach you've always wanted. With the mix of humor and wisdom that has made her beloved to her many students, she removes any shame around stagnation, and cuts right to your heart with personal stories that normalize the ebb and flow of bothering in life. Jennifer is the coach who stands in the storm alongside you. Prepare to have your excuses lovingly disarmed, one by one. Before you know it, you'll be feeling the glow of hope and taking steps toward what you really want."

LAUREN FLESHMAN, author, coach, and two-time USA champion runner

"I read this book during a *why bother* time in my life, and I'm so grateful I did! I ended the book in tears, reminded of both why I'm here on this earth and why it matters that I get my bother on. Jennifer Louden does a beautiful job of weaving together story and practical advice, which I experienced as a series of aha moments!"

ANNA GUEST-JELLEY, founder of Curvy Yoga

"A unique take on how to get out of a slump when you're stuck. *Why Bother?* will inspire you to find new and creative ways to get yourself moving again, so that you can find true happiness."

KRISTIN NEFF, PhD, associate professor at the University of Texas at Austin and author of *Self-Compassion*

"Whether we fail at something we care about, or reach the heights of success, we'll all ask ourselves 'why bother?' at some point in our lives. Jennifer Louden's book lets us explore that question as a search for meaning instead of a path to madness. She doesn't give us a map with her answers, but a compass to find our own way."

SRINIVAS RAO, creator and host of the *Unmistakable Creative* podcast and author of *Audience of One*

"Chock-full of deeply vulnerable and courageous stories, Jennifer Louden's latest book helps you understand, first and foremost, that you're not alone. And that knowledge might be one of the biggest gifts, as she guides you to discovering your own answer to 'why bother?' A riveting book."

KAREN WALROND, leadership consultant, speaker, author, attorney, and coach

"*Why Bother?* is a reclamation. With curiosity, wisdom, reverence, and grace, Jennifer Louden shows us how to transform two simple words from the ultimate expression of futility into a path back to desire and, eventually, meaning. Read it, then live it."

JONATHAN FIELDS, author and founder of Good Life Project

"Hilarious, honest, and real, Jennifer Louden is a masterful storyteller and truthteller. Read this book and take your energy back, find your thread again, and figure out how to make the most of the time you have. Jennifer Louden is your guide—back to yourself, your heart, and the reasons you're here in the first place. Listen to what she says."

SARAH PECK, CEO and founder of Startup Pregnant

why
bother?

Discover the Desire for What's Next

Jennifer Louden

why
bother?

PAGE TWO
BOOKS

Some names and identifying details have been changed to protect the privacy of individuals.

Cataloguing in publication information is available from Library and Archives Canada.
ISBN 978-1-989603-12-3 (paperback)
ISBN 978-1-989603-13-0 (ebook)

Page Two
www.pagetwo.com

Edited by Amanda Lewis
Copyedited by Crissy Calhoun
Proofread by Alison Strobel
Cover design by Peter Cocking
Interior design by Peter Cocking & Jennifer Lum
Printed and bound in Canada by Friesens
Distributed in Canada by Raincoast Books
Distributed in the US and internationally by
Publishers Group West, a division of Ingram

20 21 22 23 24   5 4 3 2 1

jenniferlouden.com

To Bob

———————————

Lovers don't just meet somewhere
They're in each other all along

RUMI

Contents

1

why bother
indeed

Asking
"Why bother?" is
inevitable. It's baked
into being human.
And it's time
to notice: *how* are
you asking the
question?

―――――――――

(1)

Why Bother Indeed

"**WHY BOTHER?**" is a pseudo-question, already answered in the negative by resignation. The *why bother* many of us know all too well insists "you can't, it's been done, it's far too late and you don't have what it takes." It uses cynicism—the planet's dying, why bother?—to bolster its case that nothing you can do really matters. It replays the good old days followed by a chorus of if onlys and everybody else can but you. It beats you up for wanting more while at the same time it discourages you by insisting there isn't any more to be had. And conveniently, *why bother* has political and corporate corruption, environmental disaster, economic injustice, and the way your brain is wired to bolster its case at every turn.

Why bother's most familiar side is a grubby bummer, defined by despair and punctuated by long sighs. It shows up as emptiness, blame, numbing out, coasting, complaining, starting something and then stopping. The desolate kind of *why bother* means looking only in the rearview mirror of your life, back at your story that no longer makes sense to you or has been taken from you. Or, if you're younger, you may find yourself looking into the future and believing all the good stuff of life is either out of your reach or no longer exists. It's letting grief over past losses and traumas devour your future. It's giving up on believing there is more for you, a *more* that can be as satisfying, as enlivening, as meaningful, as beautiful as what has come before or what has yet to be. It's choosing comfort and routine over aliveness and growth. It's believing your story of what's *not* possible more than the bracing reality of taking action. It's knowing you'll never hear the voice of your beloved partner or friend or parent again—and refusing to listen for anything else. It's too much sugar, too much wine, too many nights watching hours of TV, or too much partying when you want to be dancing or writing or learning the names of the constellations. It's pointlessness, apathy, embitterment, disappointment, dismay. Perhaps, most of all, it's disgust at yourself for being here in this haggard blank ick.

What most of us have never learned is that *why bother* is one of the most important questions we can ever ask. It's natural, even inevitable. It's baked into being human. It's the question that can drag you down or guide you to what you want, to the desire that animates and enlivens your *what's next*. It's all in how you ask.

I'm not talking about surface-level wants. There are only so many shoes, cupcakes, glasses of sauvignon blanc, and murder mysteries—as well as promotions, houses, cars, and awards—a person can enjoy before they want more out of life. And that's what we want: *more*. More satisfaction, more significance, more engagement, more intimacy, more creativity, more love, more connection, more aliveness. Your brain is wired to make meaning and it does that by constructing an ongoing narrative about why you do what you do and why it matters. Even as neuroscientists and philosophers gather to debate whether or not we have free will, whether or not we have a fixed self, and whether or not being human is the special be-all and end-all we've spent millennia convincing ourselves it is, even still, our brains seek meaning. You do that by creating a narrative. You can't turn your brain's story-making machine off.

Your mission is to create a new story that nurtures a flourishing and fulfilled future. The idea that it's just a story makes some people uneasy but when you step back, all human culture is based on a story. Democracy is a story. Marriage is a story. A company's culture is a story. Religions each have a story. What often entangles us in the desolate kind of *why bother* is being unwilling or unable to do the work of writing a new story that we can wholeheartedly love. What you want—and must have—to bother again is a story you believe in.

And lest this all sound like a shit ton of work and you're ready to shut this book and binge some *Queer Eye*, I've got great news. *You're already doing it.*

Yep. *You're already bothering again.* You're already in the process of renewal and revitalization that's built into being human, an organic creative process that, when you work with it *and* relax into it, will take you back into liveliness, zest, and enthusiasm for your real desires—or help you find them for the first time. Contrary to what you think, you're not becalmed in a *why bother* wasteland. This is not a forever state. You've answered the call and the process has already begun. Take a breath and know that bothering again is in progress and it's going to rock your world.

In my various sloughs of despair, starting in my mid-twenties, I told myself an "I failed" story—failed at screenwriting, failed at self-help, failed at marriage, failed at novel writing, failed at parenting, failed at being a good friend, failed at living fully... and on my list would go. But each of those "failures" was in fact a tale of desire denied or truncated, an opportunity to write a new story that I turned away from because I was too timid or too addicted to comfort, or I was trying to be somebody important or afraid of being broke. I did things like insist my desires look a certain way and were completed "successfully" within a totally unrealistic time frame. I forgot that the purpose of desire is to draw us forward into living, into what captivates us—not to help us attain a particular career or creative goal or get paid more or even to stay married or find lasting love. I forgot that every major transition requires rediscovering desire; without that, I faltered. I forgot that what I bother about is always my choice and that I must actually choose, instead of looking outside myself for what to do next and then pretending it was my choice.

Sometimes *what's next* involves reclaiming what has been lost. Allow me to introduce you to June. June's a composite portrait of the thousands of people who have attended my retreats and courses over the years. She is twenty-four or thirty-nine or fifty or seventy-two. At our first gathering, she's afraid, her voice shakes. "I've wanted to write (or paint or take photographs or sing or...) since I was eight years old but then..." The reasons vary. It might be the death of a parent, or being good at math and encouraged to go into engineering, or she kept writing but technical writing, or she took photos until her kids were born. Or she painted, but it wasn't as easy as she thought it would be. Or she got so much early praise, she froze. Or the patriarchal capitalist machine wore her down or taught her that what she desired was foolish. Whatever the reasons, the results are the same: something vital and important to her went underground and now she's hunting to get it back. More to the point, she's looking for *what's next*.

Sometimes *what's next* has nothing to do with lost creativity. Meet Ruby, who loved her work, loved her hobbies, was surrounded by great friends, but was asking *why bother* to stay in her twenty-five-year-long intimate partnership. Or Alex, who had worked hard to get his degrees and land a good job, but now that he had one, he found himself stalled and scared. "I did everything I was supposed to do and now I'm like, 'This is all there is?' That's so frightening to ask." Or Cathy, who had worked hard so she could retire, yet found a core part of her identity was wrapped up in her job. "Who would I be if I don't have that?" she asked. "Could I find something to do that was significant enough to be satisfying? Would I really be able to leave all this success behind without leaving myself behind too?"

Or Sam, who got through their cancer treatment and regained their health only to feel at a loss: "When I was fighting for my life, it gave me purpose, which I hadn't had for years. But when I was well again, there was *why bother* waiting for me, but now it felt even more fraught. I was alive, I'd survived, I'd better make all the suffering worth it."

Jessica found herself living a life she hated: "I was alone in a land of flat cornfields, my sacred mountains nowhere in sight. I was standing downstairs in a house that had never felt like a home despite my endless efforts to decorate. I was quarantined at home while on radioactive iodine during the final step after my thyroid cancer diagnosis. Every aspect of my life was depleting; my well was empty. I often stared around me in shock. 'How is this my life?' In one of those moments of utter disbelief, I heard a voice as clear as if someone was talking to me, 'If you stay here, you will die.'"

All of which is to say, *why bother* comes knocking no matter your age, gender identity, socio-economic circumstances, cultural heritage, or sexuality. It shows up when you need to let go of an aspect of your life or your self-image or your work—and *there is nothing that you care about yet to replace it*. There isn't a new story connected to what you desire—yet.

Why bother also shows up when there is a desire you have put aside or never attended to that is demanding your devotion—even if that desire is not clear. Finally, *why bother* appears when there is something beckoning but you don't trust yourself to explore it or perhaps don't believe you even deserve it.

You might not use the words *why bother* but instead find yourself saying, "What's the point? Who cares? Why is this all so hard?" Or some version of "wanting more is selfish, I should be grateful for what I have." Or "I'm too tired to bother again." The words vary, but the call is the same: find your desire. You will use that energy, that well of inspiration and life force, to find *what's next*, and to make meaning out of suffering. Whether you're ready to steer your life for the first time or for a fresh interpretation or recalibrating after life-changing grief, please know there is nothing the matter with you and there's no need to panic or to despair. I promise.

Here's the amazing quality of *why bother* that's essential to recognize—you need both sides of the question. Your reconnection to desire and what brings you alive can't come without the angsty blankness you feel now, just as there's no wet without dry, no light without dark, no love without loss.

We all know the usual way to ask *why bother*, which presents a foregone conclusion. That side of *why bother* is all about quitting on living. It's believing there is nothing satisfying in your future. It's saying, "No more for me." It's avoiding what's not working until you believe your avoidance is innate. It's always eating the burnt toast and pretending that's all you want. It's staying imprisoned in your golden handcuffs or your poor artist identity or your role as a mom. It's letting your family or your partner or your situation determine what you can have and do. It's being so certain that if you disrupt the status quo, no matter how leaden and stultifying it is for you, you or someone you love will perish.

But when you consider the flip side of *why bother*, you see that where you find yourself holds both resignation and longing, despair and desire, lassitude and vigor, your past and your future. When you face both sides, instead of blindly dedicating yourself to deadening apathy, existential despair, blasé pronouncements, hiding from your desires, attachment to a cherished identity, or even naive enthusiasm, you release *why bother*'s negative power. You begin to grapple with what must be invited in for you to thrive—and what must be let go of.

Asking *why bother* with honesty, admitting what you don't want to bother about anymore or never did, while opening to desire, can slice through deep layers of denial and self-abandonment, the low-grade hum of "I guess this is good enough" and "That's all there is" and "I don't dare." *Why bother* insists you start listening to what you really want. This is not selfish, and it won't make you a self-centered navel-gazer; in fact, the exact opposite will happen, in time. *Why bother* is intimately connected to how you appreciate and value yourself and to the belief that your voice and desires matter, which allows you to connect and serve in renewed ways, if you desire. Grappling with *why bother* is how you go

"The courage to continue before the face of despair is the recognition that in those eyes of darkness we find our own night vision."

TERRY TEMPEST WILLIAMS,
WHEN WOMEN WERE BIRDS

beyond your known horizon, past the familiar shape of what no longer works and is squeezing you dry, and into the fresh territory of "what if" and "I wonder." It's not an easy or gentle question, but ask a gentler question and you'll end up rearranging the deck chairs on your own *Titanic*.

I mapped out a six-stage approach to help you use both sides of the question to liberate your desire for *what's next*. I've also included all kinds of resources on my website—audio recordings, videos, reminders, journaling prompts—to delight and support you. You'll find a heads-up to those resources throughout the book or you can bookmark jenniferlouden.com/whybother and go there when you want something more.

Here's the map to getting your bother on:

1. Leave behind

Examine the excuses that you're too depressed, anxious, old, or ill, that it's too late, that you're not good enough. See with love what needs to be jettisoned so you can start a new story.

2. Ease in

Trust yourself to wonder, awaken self-compassionate grit, investigate habits that deaden possibility, and return again and again to the truth that you matter.

3. Settle

Find the stillness that makes everything else possible. Settling doesn't mean being static or putting up with less than what you desire.

4. Desire

The heart of the *why bother* approach, the missing piece in your life. Make friends with the misunderstood quality and energy of desire, replace substitute desires, drop your diversions, and be amazed.

5. Become by doing

Follow through with gentle, devoted action that helps you stay in the gap, check your head, and become the most human version of you.

6. Be seen

Celebrate your desires in community and take refuge in belonging.

These steps form a gentle, non-linear guide to finding your way to a life you are impatient to live. You won't need everything in the book and you might not start at the beginning. Trust yourself to jump in where you wish and ignore whatever doesn't serve you.

Proceed at a pace that feels safe and nurturing to you. If you are deep in grief, please know I am never suggesting you hurry up and "get over it." Life after loss, especially a life-altering loss, is never the same. *Why bother* can help you understand that while life will never be the same, it can still be beautiful and fulfilling.

Right about now is where I'm supposed to give you my story, the one that says all you have to do is follow my patented six-step process and your life will be perfect. It's the story of how on one dark day, when I was at my lowest, the miracle occurred. My clammy, mucky Job-like affliction receded, the angels fluttered around me, gilding me with glitter made from unicorn laughter, and I know without a doubt what I wanted to bother about—and how. I had my mojo back to the 10,000th power and I looked ten years younger to boot—oh, and I made millions.

Gag. That didn't happen. It does for some people—except maybe the unicorn-laughter glitter—and you will read some of their stories in these pages, but there was no miracle for me. With a lot of effort and a lot of time, I found my way back to life, to purpose, to caring. Most of all, to desire. I progressed in fits and starts. At times, I was aware I was emerging from my funk, but I often wasn't sure how or what I still needed to do. In fact, continuing to move forward rather than wanting to be finished helped me finally emerge, look around, and say, "Holy shit, I'm a different person. And I really love this person I've become. Or discovered. Or heck, rescued because she was always here."

If I can't offer you a tidy success story, what hope can I give you that life is waiting to come back to you? That life loves you? That ennui and despair are not a permanent state? How about a list? On the left is me during the lowest point in my longest *why bother* period—because of course I've experienced more than one—and on the right is me now.

Creatively defeated	Creatively determined
Self-judging	Welcoming all my experiences
Shoulda woulda coulda	What can I make, enjoy, savor starting now?
Busy but unfulfilled	Patiently asking, "What do I really want?"
Crippling back ailment	Pain-free and strong
Dithering and half-assing	Fully committed
Envious	Able to wish others well (almost always)
Crabby, judgmental, cynical	Taking a stand for joy and steady, inspired action
"Nobody likes me"	The agent of my belonging
Waiting for permission	Giving myself permission

The big difference, and one I will guide you through, is that I've crafted a solid foundation of how to bother. I can stand on it, bounce on it, check in with it. It's part of me now. *I know how to keep getting my bother on.* And a big part of that foundation was learning everything is not fixable. I used to believe if I simply meditated enough, prayed enough, went to therapy enough, ate clean enough, got successful enough, I would stop suffering. And bonus point: I would also never suffer again. I believed that this very natural human condition was something that needed to be solved by my continual efforts. When my life really hit the skids when I was forty-five and I couldn't keep my marriage or save my dad's life or write more books, *why bother* took my spirit by the neck like my terrier does his toys and shook it hard. Surrendering to the truth that I couldn't fix much, and I truly didn't need to try, freed me from the terrible conviction that something was fundamentally wrong with me, which is the belief that had kept me most imprisoned in the land of the lost.

I also spent far too many years lost because I didn't know how normal and important these loss-of-desire passages are and because I didn't have a way to name them and work with them. I was so ashamed to be questioning everything and finding so little satisfying. So ashamed to not love my life every single moment—and myself. So ashamed to be fantasizing about disappearing. I had no idea that desire goes underground for many reasons: because we're afraid to try for what we want, because we constantly hate on ourselves, because the mainstream culture tries to sell us an empty crappy story we could care less about, because we age out of a desire, because we complete something, because something

Loss of Desire Looks Like This

Self-hatred · Life-altering loss · Trauma

Racism · Illness · Anticipated loss

Divorce · Job loss · Financial stress

Toxic boss or workplace

Creative shaming and disappointments

Being denied, blocked, dismissed

Exhaustion · Raising kids

Overwork to keep wolf from the door

Overwork as a habit or identity

Complaining too long without taking action

Having or believing you
have to do everything all alone

Denying what you want as a matter of routine

Following the rules no matter what

———————————

is taken from us, because we've learned what we need to learn, because we're exhausted, because we've stayed too long in a job or relationship or identity, because we've put everyone else first forever, because we never had the agency or resources to ask, "What do I want?" All of these can dent, scatter, and demean our desire, and without it, we lack the energy to look on the other side of *why bother.*

Not long before my marriage to my first husband failed and I plunged into the darkest years of my life, my close friend Ann and I had a prophetic conversation on our weekly walk. We walked around our tiny island downtown, past where we bought our eyeglasses and past the florist whose flowers had festooned all the major occasions of our lives. We stopped to admire the orchids crowding the window as I offhandedly recounted a story about a coach I'd met recently at a conference in Denver.

"Ooh la la," Ann said, looking from the orchids to me, her hazel eyes comically wide.

"What?" I said, as we crossed the street in front of the big white Congregational church and headed down the hill toward Eagle Harbor, the ferry horn cutting through the damp cool afternoon.

"Sounds like he was flirting with you."

I yanked on Ann's jacket sleeve and snorted. "As if."

She gave me her Ann look, a sort of laser-eyed but loving stare.

I busied myself waving at a friend driving by in her silent Prius. There was something I didn't like about this conversation, but I wasn't sure what. I tried to change the subject by chattering about a new restaurant that was supposed to be going in the building we are walking by. Ann ignored my tactic.

"You sounded excited talking about him," she said. "Energized."

"I don't flirt," I said. "I stopped flirting when I married Chris eighteen years ago."

We clattered out on the boardwalk that skirted the marina. There were mostly sailboats docked and a handful of fishing boats and tugs. The breeze smelled of tar, diesel, and fish and chips from the pub.

Ann was waiting for me to say more. She was great at silently waiting. "I used to be so easily flattered," I finally said. "I never could hold my own against men, stand up for what I wanted. When I got married, not flirting, not being around men much, it was safer." I suddenly sensed how little I knew how to trust what I wanted or how to stand up for it, but I shook that off. It couldn't possibly be true. I was self-employed, I guided women to be truer to themselves, I meditated. Dammit, I led a courageous life.

"What do you think it costs you, not letting any of that vital energy in?" Ann asked.

"Nothing." My tone was almost belligerent. I bumped gently into her, a little hip check to signal I wasn't mad. "I settled down, grew up. That's what people are supposed to do."

"But one of the things you often say on our walks is how you are the one who has to handle everything, keep it together," she said. "I wonder what the cost is to you, of doing that, when you're also cutting off the energy of desire?"

"Are you telling me to have an affair?" We turned up the hill again, the wind cold at our backs.

"You know I'm not. But I am curious. That much energy, it has to go somewhere."

I wanted to tell her she was reading too much Jung, that everything didn't come down to the unconscious. We reached her Volvo. The ferry had let out and the island's hourly pattern traffic pulsed by: bicyclists, heads down, trying to beat the motorcycles and the cars; then the motorcyclists roaring by, leaving a trail of exhaust, defeating the cyclists every time; then the cars accelerating up the hill or turning into town. I hugged Ann.

"I love that you want me to be vital."

She held me at arm's length. "What if you let yourself stop doing and taking care of everybody and just listened to what you want? You could come stay at my house. Let everything else go for a little bit. You could just see what happens when you stop trying to hold everything together and let yourself want." She squeezed my shoulders.

I imagined being in Ann's guest room, being quiet long enough and deep enough to understand what I wanted without distracting myself with another project or taking care of Mom or my daughter or money stuff. I could be still long enough for something important that had forever alluded my jumping-bean mind to snap into view.

"There are a hundred thousand species of love, separately invented, each more ingenious than the last, and every one of them keeps making things."

RICHARD POWERS, THE OVERSTORY

But I was already saying no. Saying something jaunty and false about being the one who held things together, I had a young child, I earned the money, that's just the way it was. But even as I said it, I knew I was hiding from something. My whole body wanted to go home with her right then and there and have her tuck me into bed in her little guest room. I wanted to let feeling I had to be an adult and take care of everything and everybody roll off me. I wanted to dig into the feeling there was more waiting for me if I would just let *more* become clear.

Instead I skittered across the street in a break between the cars. "See you next week!"

Ann yelled across Winslow. "Think about it, at least?"

"I will!" I yelled back and hurried around the corner, where my bravado promptly drained away. I trudged to my car, suddenly so tired I wasn't sure I could drive the three miles home. I was blank, couldn't even remember what it was Ann had offered, but it had sounded so delicious. I had never wanted something so much.

The next morning Ann sent me this poem by Ko Un:

It is said that nothing can become new
unless it first turns to ashes.
For a whole decade,
my misfortune was not having turned to ashes.
Burning a mound of dead leaves in late autumn
  I want to weep.

I sobbed as I read the poem, knowing I had missed so many opportunities to burn what needed to be turned to ash and that I would most likely miss this one too. I could practically see all my younger selves, in a kind of queue, turning away from what needed to be turned to ash and settling for what she thought she could have.

When I look back at those moments, I see a woman who had no idea how to heed the stirrings of *why bother*, no idea how to pause and get curious, to wonder, to let in desire; I feel no shame, only great compassion. There wasn't anything wrong with me, nor is there anything wrong with you.

We don't have enough stories about the cyclical nature of flowing and not flowing, caring and not caring, living with purpose and being bewildered, making stuff and not making anything except our morning coffee, living full of desire and not knowing what desire even is. We do not have enough stories of how making a life that feels good and alive is a never-ending process of reinvention, of putting together a bit of this and a bit of that, of having something work for a while and then grind to a halt or be taken from us or simply lose its juice. Of muddling around until we find our way through.

My muddling-around times weren't all bad, not without interest or growth. Which is exactly what can be tricky: not all lost or blah times are easy to label. We circle and spiral and there are polka dots of "this feels good." It's not being able to put our finger on what's not right, but then being sure we've found it, then doubting ourselves again. Or as I came to think of it, there would be no clear finish line, no marching band. Instead, there would be a slow-growing sense of rightness and satisfaction.

My intention with this book is to offer you companionship, not prescription, because that's what I needed most in my low time when I only knew how to ask *why bother* in an enervating way. I needed someone to remind me, again and again, that my experience was normal and inevitable, part of the creative process of making a life. I needed someone to startle me out of my stories of how it was too late, I'd blown it, and I didn't have any energy left to begin again. I needed someone to remind me that even though my life would never be the same—my father wasn't coming back from the dead, my mom would not recover from Alzheimer's, my first marriage was well and truly over—and my creative and spiritual faith were gutted, there would be a new life, a different life, *if I allowed it*.

Once I discovered that I could stop my endless circling back on myself and notice how much I cared about following my desires, I discovered I always knew how to bother! So do you. It would take you a month of twelve-hour days to list all the ways you have cared, nurtured, encouraged, and created in your life. There are so many ways and situations right now where you bother very much. Even in the worst of times, I never stopped bothering about my kids or my dogs or my friends. (And probably not my hair, except that period when I dyed it almost black and liked that it made me look half-dead.) My point is you have a massive built-in capacity to care. You can trust that. You can, and will, use it.

Lay down the myth that where you find yourself is a penalty for screwing up or giving up. Stop asking, "Why me?" Why not you? Suffering and loss build our connection to each other. They hone what matters. You can also stop thinking that you have to figure out your *why bother* once and for all. Rilke wrote, "May what I do flow from me like a river, / no forcing and no holding back." These lines tell us how to live, how to bother again, to trust the creativity that animates everything. Rivers are never done. Even after they flow into the sea, they are still moving, discovering, unfolding.

That's why I wrote this book: to remind you to allow life in. It's not all up to you, but you have to dip a toe or two into the river; you have to allow that something can be different. I'm holding out my hand. I'll walk into the river with you. I promise the water is more than fine.

What's
next is code
for loving
life again and
letting life
love you.

———

(2)

Still Need Convincing?

_____

RIGHT ABOUT NOW you may be thinking, "Sure, I care about my relationships or my faith or my health, but that's not what's missing. I want to care about *what's next*—what I might make or build or write or contribute."

Fair enough.

But what I've found is if you go in search of a specific *what's next*, you short-circuit the renewal you need. *What's next* is not a destination; it's not about your career or a cause or a community or creative work. It might involve those things, but *what's next* is so far beyond any of those. *What's next* is whole-hearted contact and immersion in life. *What's next* is to become more human, or as Stephen Colbert said in an interview with Anderson Cooper, "What's the point of being here and being human if you can't be the most human you can be?"

What's next is code for loving life again and letting life love you. You might have another name for it: God's love, Source, Presence, basic goodness, nature, Gaia, Shiva and Shakti. I'll use "life" because it's neutral and because, in my experience, life yearns to be expressed fully and joyfully. Life is bubbling away, saying, "Take me, use me, live me." And I've found it takes an awful lot of effort to turn our back on it.

"Nah," you might say, "I'm good. I'm doing enough. I really do desire this life on the couch, and I know I'd fail that exam regardless, and everything is downhill from here anyway. You need to know when to bow out, Jen."

That may be, but why not take this little quiz and see which of these statements ring true for you, if any? Because there may be some clear signs that it's time for you to bother—again or for the first time. Give it a try; check off any statements that apply to you.

☐ You drag yourself through the day waiting until you can put on your sweats, make a bowl of popcorn, and binge-watch your favorite show.

☐ You look forward to getting into bed more than getting out.

☐ You hear the call of something you want and then zip in the opposite direction.

☐ You know something has to change, but you keep pretending it doesn't.

☐ You've spent most of your life caring about what others told you mattered, and now those concerns and pursuits don't cut it, but you don't know what does.

☐ You want to go deep with something you care about, but you have no role models nor any guarantee it will be worth it, so you waffle or give up.

☐ You tell yourself to toughen up, get a spine, look at what Mother Teresa or your personal role model did.

☐ You have no idea how to move forward in creating a life that sustains you without turning it into another burdensome item on your endless to-do list.

☐ You want someone else to tell you exactly how to care again, in precise instructions with clear diagrams.

☐ You can't help but give others advice, but you rarely listen to your own.

☐ You keep dismissing what brings you delight and meaning because it isn't a "big enough" deal or won't earn you more money.

☐ The "what if" committee is running your life and blocking every move you might make.

☐ You are sure you can't withstand another heartbreak.

☐ You intimately know your disappointments and failures but can't recall your moments of learning and soaring.

☐ You've been on the same hamster wheel for so long all you can imagine is running yourself into a worn-out nub while listening to the screech of the wheel spinning.

☐ Every third sentence out of your mouth is a complaint.

☐ You never complain because you're conditioned to just take it and take it and take it.

☐ You worry a chronic illness prevents you from ever having the energy to bother again.

☐ You mostly eat food that makes you feel like shit.

☐ You have two or three glasses of wine in the evening and then rarely have the energy or focus to do what you want the next day.

☐ You keep putting yourself into debt by bailing out other people or buying things you don't really want or need.

☐ You don't get your regular health exams.

☐ You feel trapped and drained by your success and say things like, "I want to get back to why I started this in the first place."

☐ You threw yourself heart-first into a project and it went great and it's barely a minute later and people are already asking, "What's next?" and it makes you so, so tired.

☐ You spend your free time looking at other people's lives and perfect houses and sparkling gowns at award ceremonies and wishing desperately you were one of them.

☐ You endlessly replay what so-and-so did to you and tell yourself because of that you're screwed forever and can't do what you want.

☐ It's futile to bother because some guy will dismiss you, mansplain you, or you will otherwise hit a glass ceiling.

☐ You tell yourself that once your partner/child/best friend/dog is all taken care of, then you will look at what you want.

☐ Staying comfortable is your biggest priority.

☐ The dire state of the planet squeezes all the desire out of you.

☐ You are 10,000,000 percent certain there is nothing interesting or engaging possible for you ever again.

If you checked off any of these statements, please read on. Taking stock of your life isn't comfortable and that's why most of us avoid it. But eventually the cost of avoidance becomes too high a price to pay. Even if reading that checklist made you look away because you can't bear to know what's happening, you've already ripped the bandage off. Savor that. It's proof you are in the process. Now let's keep going.

Getting your *why bother* on means giving despair the middle finger.

———

(3)

Savor versus Serve

OBSTINATELY BELIEVE LIFE can get better no matter what, and I believe in the power of always beginning again. I believe in life as a limitless force, pushing us to create and regenerate. I believe life hungers to live through us. I believe in fighting for your life.

My optimistic nature is the way I'm built, and it results from having had, despite my share of challenges, a very privileged life. I am white, cisgender, straight, able-bodied, and was raised in the US. I've never had to worry about where my next meal would come from, if I could pay my utility bills, or whether I would be shot because of the color of my skin. I've had basic health insurance most of my adult life. While there were plenty of years when I didn't allow myself to buy a latte, let alone go on vacation, I never worried I would be homeless.

I tell you this because the challenges to bothering again are internal and external, and your external challenges may be a hell of a lot more daunting than mine. My white privilege and socio-economic privilege have meant I had the basic support we all need, and that's a very important factor in my coming around. The idea we are solely responsible for our well-being and success is a lie, one that allows governments and corporations to dodge their roles in supporting people. It's a lie that leaves too many of us feeling invisible, frustrated, and alienated because we think we should be able to make a good, safe, prosperous life all on our own. Nobody does and nobody ever has.

Bothering again is about you and how you see what's possible, but it's also about your environment, the support you have or don't have, the systems that oppress you or ignore you. Being the agent of your life is critical to bothering again, but so is recognizing how the world is failing you. I won't be suggesting you think your way to adequate wages or affordable health care because that's one of the ways to bury yourself even deeper in the pointless, draining side of *why bother*. Which is to say, there are big forces working against us—from the way our brains are wired to the climate crisis—but don't count us humans out yet. And we want to check that we haven't counted ourselves out by reflexively choosing cynicism.

Because when you choose cynicism, whether in response to your own dreams or to the state of the world, you are convincing yourself it's far smarter to opt out instead of getting hurt. Cynicism is perfectionism wrapped in self-protection disguised as world-weary experience. You say, "If the future can't be exactly the way I want it, and if I can't know my efforts will be meaningful, I'll give up now. I won't even try. I'd rather disappoint myself now than be disappointed later." You also buy in to the status-quo story that nothing ever really gets better, so why bother. Cynicism feels smart, righteous, efficient—in a cynical mindset, I don't have to dig into the subtleties of an issue, nor do I have to work to get to know people; I can avoid.

I had fallen into cynicism about issues I care about, like the climate crisis. I just didn't believe my efforts were making a difference. That's the assumption cynicism helps us jump to: that our efforts toward political, environmental, and social change must either produce measurable results we can point to, or we have failed completely. But that is a Hollywood version of change, not how real change has ever happened. Change is often agonizingly slow and astonishingly complex. You can rarely, if ever, point to any one event or protest or opinion piece and say, "That's what did it." But we often insist on knowing that what we did counted, that it moved the needle, and even more so in our Twitter-finger times. If we aren't guaranteed immediate results, we give up.

It's easy to confuse being cynical with being skeptical. Skepticism is healthy questioning, a willingness to keep an open mind while researching, asking hard questions, looking at both sides of an issue, and experimenting. Healthy skepticism acknowledges there are crooked people, bad ideas, Facebook posts you shouldn't have shared, and politicians who lie multiple times a day. But healthy skeptics do not automatically reject everything that doesn't fit their view of the world. Healthy skepticism takes work, a lot of work, while naive cynicism assumes it knows everything. Naive cynicism is, frankly, lazy and allows the status quo, which oppresses too many of us, to persist.

Being cynical cuts you off from caring, confirms your view of the world without question, and can become a self-perpetuating loop—you trust other people less and take less action on what you care about since nothing you do matters. Cynicism can keep you firmly in the windowless, airless side of *why bother*.

You may veer into the swampland of cynicism or *why bother*—or both—because you've bothered *so* much, because you've hoped and prayed and worked your butt off and it either hasn't seemed to be effective or you've burned out. You care ardently about so many things: survivors of war and sexual violence in South Sudan, food insecurity in Haiti, Black people being gunned down by police, the Great Pacific garbage patch, elephants poached for their tusks, the Earth collapsing. *Why bother* is a personal and a collective mood, and the collective mood affects you. Compassion fatigue, information overwhelm, powerlessness in the face of bureaucracy, institutional racism, sexism, the climate crisis, and giant-scale corruption—there are a zillion excellent reasons to feel defeated and that your efforts are futile.

But when we are idling in the despair zone, we forget that the very nature of life is change. Things don't always change for the better, and you often don't know what role you played when they do. When you focus on what didn't work or believe what you did wasn't enough, you wipe out any feelings of efficacy and your ability to get off the couch along with it.

Getting your *why bother* on is not a selfish act; it's giving despair the middle finger. It's saying you *do* have power, there is a reason to act, life does and can change for the better, and it's time to find a sustainable way to care. You're ready to jettison despair and cynicism and the all-or-nothing need to save the world, all of which can keep you stuck in the *why bother* doldrums.

I've seen it countless times in friends and in the people I've coached. The desire to make a difference at first fuels purpose but then takes over her entire life, leading to burnout, pessimism, and sometimes illness. Unable to give in the same way she has in the past, yet certain she must or else she is failing, she stops doing much of anything, including what brings her alive and gives her pleasure. Making a measurable difference becomes the only way for her to construct a meaningful life; anything else is shallow and selfish. And every time her desire to care stirs to life, with it comes the stern belief that whatever she does must count in a big way. But this is what burned her out in the first place. So she stops and lapses back into indifference, even as it drives her batty with boredom and purposelessness.

Or here's the same scenario in a different outfit: judging yourself for not making enough of a contribution. Since you're lazy and selfish for not saving the world, you're not allowed to do what's calling you unless you are certain it will save the world. Elegant watertight trap, isn't it? You quit before you start. Nothing ever has a chance to develop, to grow, to become.

Then there's the convincing idea that it's all too big. Where would you even start? You work for a nonprofit, you donate money to charities and recycle and bike to work, so what else are you to do? Isn't that enough? You're just one person!

It takes some parsing, this wanting to make the world better. We know focusing only on ourselves leaves us feeling hollow. We know there's no justice in us having safe drinking water and flush toilets, for one small example, while billions of people don't. We know the climate crisis is tipping away from us and our efforts are urgently needed. But when pointlessness and lassitude stain our days, it's time to examine our stories of what we should do or could do, so we can find what's ours to do now.

You need a story that motivates you, one that is linked to what matters to you and that recognizes the world doesn't rely on *you* to spin on its axis. Balancing our need to help with our humanity is about humility and self-regard. You're not the only one with the ability to fix a particular problem, but dismissing your efforts as too little or too flawed is equally absurd. When you know why you bother, your aspiration to heal and help arises naturally.

In my *why bother* time, I turned to service to haul myself out. I wanted to build a bridge between self-care—what I had been writing about and teaching for fifteen years—and service. I was trying to transmute my cynicism about self-care being turned into a multi-billion-dollar industry. As E.B. White wrote, "I arise in the morning torn between a desire to improve (or save) the world and a desire to enjoy (or savor) the world. This makes it hard to plan the day." I renamed my business "savor and serve," but I couldn't get traction on my new mission. I lacked a way to frame the connection between "savor" and "serve" that would be compelling to people who felt like they had already served enough. Turns out, I wanted savor and serve to save me, to give me a reason to bother again. I was looking for something outside of me to give me purpose. And let's be honest: I also wanted to look good doing it.

I saw my folly when I was a week away from taking my daughter, Lillian, sixteen at the time, and myself to Kolkata, India, to work in an orphanage. I would do leadership training for the staff, and she would teach soccer and hang out with the kids. It was on my list to buy plane tickets the same day I happened to chat with a dear friend who had grown up in India. She gently but urgently told me how difficult a month in the summer in Kolkata would be and got me to question what real impact Lilly and I could have. I can still feel the heat in my face as I realized what I was doing: using the time and energy of the director of the orphanage to help me design a way to feel useful—oh, and give my daughter something cool to write her college essay about. I hung up and emailed the director to apologize, then donated the amount of money I would have spent on the trip to the orphanage. Lilly wrote an essay that came from her own experience, rather than one her mom tried to manufacture for her, and I learned that a sustainable and true *why bother* wasn't going to come from attempting to "save" someone else and certainly not from trying to look good but from deep inside me.

Serving others is part of what makes a meaningful life. So is remembering that positive change has happened, will happen, is happening in the world. *You can't bother if you buy into the despair narrative.* But when service and working for the greater good becomes a "should" or a joyless burden or a way to prove ourselves worthy, we've confused being of service with being a savior or with saving ourselves. We don't need to be saved and neither does anybody else.

What would it be like to step away from thinking you know how you must help or how your help will impact the world? To give up predetermining what being of service looks like? Can you leave behind the desire to save the world, recognize the truth that you cannot, and yet stop dismissing the efforts you do make?

Activist and author Parker Palmer writes, "One of the most important qualities a person can have in our time—a person who wants to make this a better world—is the capacity to 'stand in the tragic gap' between corrosive cynicism and irrelevant idealism, between what is and could be. We need the inner strength to hold both the reality and our hope at the same time."

We need the inner strength to accept our limits and to serve in ways that serve us and others. We need to stop trying to be heroes. We need to stop buying the story we're all screwed.

As you work on finding your individual *why bother*, how might going after what you savor now allow you to serve later? After getting my bother on, what naturally arose for me, little by little, was a deep desire to work to avert the climate crisis. My cynicism and exhaustion fell away. I was able, as Buddhist teacher Joanna Macy says, to let my heart be broken by the state of the world. Before, I averted my eyes from everything that made me sad or enraged. I told myself I wasn't strong enough to do enough—that what I did had to be big, all or nothing, or it didn't count. Now I root myself in savoring and gratitude, and trust that my small actions can be useful and fit my talents. This approach paradoxically frees my energy to do more, to truly savor and serve.

Every act of self-harshness stoppers the flow of life and creativity that brings you to *what's next.*

(4)

Take Stock

BEFORE YOU CAN begin to bother, you must cut yourself some slack. Every act of self-harshness stoppers the flow of life and creativity that brings you to *what's next*. Every time you insist you should be further along by now, or wish you had a different past, or otherwise judge yourself, you build a stronger barrier between you and why bother. Self-forgiveness and self-acceptance poke holes in that barrier and can, eventually, dismantle it entirely.

Back when I hugged my mistakes close and used them as proof of my inherent badness and the reasons I wasn't worthy of loving life, you could have tried anything to get me to believe I could forgive and accept myself and I would have politely pretended to agree with you. As more than one person pointed out to me in those years, "You've written books about being kind to yourself. Maybe you should read one of them."

I knew how hard I was being on myself, but running my mind over my mistakes and recounting all the ways I wasn't good enough made me feel safe. If I relaxed my guard, I believed I would immediately screw up again—and worse than before.

And even when I moved forward and tried to bother again—writing more books, creating new courses, leading retreats, coaching people who were doing interesting stuff, learning to be a better parent, remodeling a house—I second-guessed almost everything I did. I created a new course based on one of my books that received rave reviews... and then never offered it again. I started so many different books and abandoned them, not because they were bad ideas but because I could not believe in myself. I would answer email for an hour instead of playing with Lilly and then beat myself up.

If you called a dear friend today and asked, "Do you see me being unduly hard on myself?" and "Do you think that might hinder my future?" what might your friend reflect back to you? I know my friends would have shouted, "Yes and please, for god's sake, stop it!"

One day, when I caught myself self-hating, I paused and genuinely asked myself, "What's good here right now?" Then I kept asking. Little by little, I experienced the pain of taking myself out of life *at the same time* I let in the good of my dog's wet nose; of Lilly tripping in the front door after school, calling out, "Where are you, Mama?"; of laughing in the driveway with my neighbors; of reading a good book. I kept catching myself in the choice to be closed off from life and then opening up, and it began to sink in: nobody was holding me hostage but me.

Roberta's turning point came when she began to forgive herself for staying in an abusive relationship. "Even after I got free, I beat myself up for staying. It took a lot of learning about how abuse and gaslighting works to understand it wasn't my fault." Jack's self-forgiveness came when he understood it wasn't his fault he got cancer. "I made the mistake of going to a healer who told me it was my thinking that caused my cancer. I knew she was full of shit but, my god, it played on my mind for so long." Jen found self-kindness through writing after she left her fiancé when he betrayed her. "My writing is a constant companion and sounding board. I am truly held, heard, and led by my own voice." Jeb turned the corner when he forgave his business partner for bankrupting their cabinet company by stealing money from their clients to buy drugs. "I knew things weren't right, but I wouldn't face it. I hid from what was happening by staying busy building cabinets. I told myself I was no good with money. Forgiving him—and forgiving myself—I had to or I would have never been able to start to rebuild my life."

You can't will yourself to accept and forgive yourself, just like you can't will yourself to love yourself. If you've spent months or years replaying mistakes or wishing things could be different, or you're recovering from trauma, it will take time for your brain and your heart to believe it's safe to move on. Take self-forgiveness on as an experiment, not a task to check off and complete. Experiment with any practices of self-forgiveness that appeal to you and see if they help. Notice if little by little you are walking away from seeing the past with unforgiving eyes and putting your gaze on what's good in the here and now. When you ask, "What's good here right now?" hold both the awareness of where you might not allow the good in—*too intense, waiting for the other shoe to drop, you don't deserve it*—and the awareness of what feels good. No need to strain or manufacture the good; it's more effective to take in what genuinely feels good in the moment. Not an ideal but the reality.

Asking "What's good here right now?" can also soften the anger and pain of circumstances beyond your control. You lost a job, a house, a partner, a child, your health, a dream. Letting the goodness of life touch you and remind you that even though frustrating and heartbreaking things have happened that you don't get to do over, there is good here now. And that can awaken new possibilities in you. Stopping to take in the good doesn't change the hard; it allows the good to live alongside the hard.

Want journaling prompts to explore self-forgiveness? Pop over to jenniferlouden.com/whybother.

You know when someone says something you've heard a thousand times before, but they word it differently or you hear it differently? I was in the middle of a seven-day meditation retreat with Richard Miller, founder of iRest, when he said, "We are doing the best we know how at the time." *At the time*. I bet my jaw dropped. Before when someone said to me,

"You were doing the best you knew how," I would always think, "No, I wasn't." Hearing *at the time* reminded me that while I had all my blind spots and biases and cultural influences, I was doing my best. When I replay something I could have done differently, whether from five years or five minutes ago, I put my hand on my heart and remind myself, "I was doing the best I knew how *at the time*."

Tammy's moment of taking stock happened in the middle of the night:

> My life was spiraling out of control, my anxiety at an all-time high. I didn't know who I was or what I believed anymore. I was using vodka and chardonnay to manage the anxiety. But it was no longer working. I couldn't imagine giving up the alcohol, the one reliable (albeit temporary) balm that had been giving me some relief. But I also knew I couldn't keep living the life I was living. It wasn't just the emotional wreckage, but I had also wrecked my digestive tract with drinking and I frequently had spontaneous rectal bleeding a total buzzkill!
>
> A doctor prescribed anti-anxiety meds and recommended I quit drinking to figure out what I was numbing. This, combined with my health concerns, were my rock bottom. "Why bother?" was definitely a question I was asking myself. I didn't know if I had it in me to continue trying. I was strongly considering plan B, which was ending it all. Then an acquaintance died by suicide and I was faced with the reality of the pain her decision had created. Now I had no options whatsoever. So I took the fucking anti-anxiety pill.

Yes, it was *just* an anti-anxiety med. But it represented so much to me. It wasn't who I wanted to be. I was as hopeless as I'd ever been in my life. I went to bed that night praying and begging to whatever it was I didn't believe in for a solution.

In the middle of the night, I sat straight up in bed. As cliché as it sounds, I saw a veil. The veil parted and on the other side was hope, possibility, and vibrancy. I knew I wanted what was on the other side. Right then I committed to doing whatever it took to live my life vibrantly.

Good thing I didn't know what it would take. Because it took everything I had. But I would not change a thing. My *why bother* list is massively long today.

Petra got a double dose of taking stock. The first happened after her father-in-law's girlfriend Moria dropped dead wrapping Christmas presents.

I was not enormously close to Moria. But we had been neighbors for sixteen years, and I knew much of her relationship with my father-in-law was often abusive, emotionally and physically. She stayed because she believed that deep down he loved her, despite his appalling behavior. She knew more than most people about my marriage issues and other challenges.

The funeral took a long time to come because there was much to sort out. My mother-in-law turned up, even though she hated Moria, and there were drunken scenes. It was all hugely undignified. About a week later, I was driving from the city to our small town and I started crying in a way I had not cried for years. I got home and said to my husband I had to do something. I had to kick-start a career, in the city. It was his turn to support me. My *why bother* was seeing Moria, dead on the floor. Someone who believed her sacrifice was worth it— and it was so clear it wasn't. I realized I had to do something— that I was sinking in this life that was so depressing, so pulling me down, and so not what I wanted out of life.

Petra pursued her career and months later started working at an Apple retail store and found herself thriving. Shortly after, her husband confessed he was a serial adulterer, but by this time Petra had enough of her own life going to survive the divorce and all the related heartache and expense.

How has your reckoning shown up? Take pen to paper and write or doodle how you've been called to bother anew. Or make a collage. Or ask a friend to listen to your story without interrupting. Start telling your new story, the way that Tammy and Petra have crafted their own stories. It's not about making something for others: it's about hearing what you know—you know more about what's next than you're aware of. *Why bother* is a foggy state, and storytelling cuts through the fog. Telling your story of waking up—even if you don't think you have a story or don't know what that story is—builds a bulwark against slipping backward.

Whatever has brought you here is asking you to let desire win out. *This is your work now.* Not your toxic boss that rightfully drives you mad, not your mother's illness, not your children's love lives, not making enough extra money to pay

"Forgiveness doesn't sit there like a pretty boy in a bar. Forgiveness is the old fat guy you have to haul up a hill."

———————

CHERYL STRAYED,
TINY BEAUTIFUL THINGS

down your debt, not saving your marriage, not finding a partner, none of it.

Your work is not about figuring out the external, whatever
that is or will be. That's a red herring, something your mind
may want to fixate on that isn't important. Your work is to
settle down, to listen, to discern what matters to you now and
to be brave enough to move toward it. To look for the daring
bright beauty in your *why bother* instead of the life-denying,
heart-shrinking shrug.

Your work is to know we humans close ourselves off from
life; life never closes itself off from us. Your work is to rediscover the unchanging goodness at your core that never leaves
you. Your work is to blow on the embers of your longings and
to trust the dignity of your desires.

I wish someone had told me that opening to life again is
my choice. I wish someone had told me I have what it takes
within me to create a new life. I wish someone had told me all
this, not once but again and again.

Can you hear me telling you?

2

the stages of bothering

You're brilliant
at self-protection,
not self-
sabotage. It's
time to know the
difference.

———————

(5)

Leave Behind

NOW THAT YOU'VE recognized the importance and power of asking "Why bother?", it's time to get your bother on. We'll start with stage one, which is about recognizing and letting go of what's keeping you stuck in the enervating side of *why bother*. You aren't denying the challenges you face or thinking it's all up to you to change but looking more closely at how your stories might need some untangling. Leaving behind is an ongoing process that starts now.

Your Emotional Immune System Is Brilliant

Bothering again unfolds in swoops and loops, piercing clarity followed by groggy stupor, confidence served with a side of self-doubt, lethargy stealing in to cover your creative joy.

If bothering again is a natural creative process, why do we complicate it by hanging on to what no longer serves us or never did? Why do we hang on to our beliefs and fears and resentments that block the way to what's next? Do we do this because we are afraid of success? Resistant to being happy? Certain we are too broken or damaged to have more of what we want? Because it's impossible to change?

None of the above! You do it because, like the rest of us, you're brilliant at keeping yourself defended. You're incredibly skilled at self-protection, at managing your emotional immune system, the purpose of which is the same as your physical immune system: reject what threatens, no matter the cost. Your emotional immune system rejects anything that threatens to leave you exposed. As Robert Kegan and Lisa Laskow Lahey note in *Immunity to Change*, "It is not change by itself that makes us uncomfortable; it is not even change that involves taking on something very difficult. Rather, it is change that leaves us feeling defenseless before the dangers we 'know' to be present that cause us anxiety."

You are afraid of being defenseless in a dangerous, frightening world. You are a mammal, and your brain and nervous system evolved to keep you safe, not to help you live a meaningful life. That you will always have an emotional immune system and it will always try to keep you defended is a key idea in unlocking how to bother again. Your goal will be to *learn how to make yourself feel safer* in order to move forward in creating a more expansive life, one that allows in new ideas and possibilities. Staying safe when you're on the blah side of *why bother* often means giving up or coasting. Staying safe when you're working the bright side of *why bother* is all about linking security and action.

The good news is your emotional immune system often hides your desires behind what Kegan and Lahey call "competing commitments." You often do the exact opposite of what you say you want to do, or even think you want to try, as a way to take care of your natural anxiety. Do any of these sound familiar?

- You start to write a novel and then throw your hat in the ring for a promotion that means working longer days and weekends.

- You decide to address your digestive issues and then go to the store and somehow buy everything that makes you bloat and feel poorly.

- You realize nothing will change for you without more sleep and you commit to good sleep hygiene and then stay up until one in the morning watching gruesome police procedurals on TV while arguing politics with trolls on Twitter.

- You give yourself a deadline to choose a grad school and then blow past it because you can't stop researching your options.

- You decide you want to spend more time in nature but keep "forgetting" to ask anyone to hike or camp with you and then you don't go alone because you're afraid.

- You want to be more intimate with your partner and book a romantic weekend away only to spend the days golfing without her and inviting people you've just met to dine with the two of you.

- You make it a goal to save money by not signing up for any more courses, trainings, or seminars and find yourself enrolled in the most expensive training yet.

It's like in *The Wizard of Oz* when Toto pulls back the curtain and everybody sees the Wizard pulling on his levers. He snatches the curtain around him, keeps talking through his machine, insisting, "Pay no attention to that man behind the curtain!" Your emotional immune system does *not* want you to see behind the curtain, but that's exactly what you have to do in this phase. Pull back the curtain and look straight at the Wizard, instead of letting it fall again and continuing to believe life is pointless.

As I mentioned before, writing this book made me aware that I want to bother about the climate crisis in a renewed way. I'd always been an ardent environmentalist, but in the last few years I'd fallen into *why bother*, given that the global situation is so terrifying. It became easier to be comfortably numb. I'd take a little action—post on social media about which kind of toilet paper doesn't use virgin wood pulp, skip eating meat and dairy, arrange my business schedule to fly less—and then get scared and stop. *But I didn't know I was scared.* Instead, I

"Resilience is born by grounding yourself in your own loveliness."

GREGORY BOYLE, TATTOOS ON THE HEART

---

would think I was waiting to get clear on how to better help, or that I was too busy with teaching, or that whatever I did was pointless, so why bother?

When I'm reaching for or in the middle of a competing commitment, I've learned to soothe myself—put my hand on my heart, lengthen my exhale to calm my nervous system, and check in. "What am I telling myself? What am I doing instead of what I say I want to do?" Now here's the crucial bit: I don't force myself to do anything different. I don't stop watching *Grantchester* and go to a 350.org meeting. I soothe and care for myself *while being aware of my thoughts and fears.* If I'm naturally moved to do something different afterward, great, but the point is the soothing and noticing.

By interrupting the moment of contraction with self-touch, longer exhales, welcoming sensation, and kind self-talk, you're teaching yourself you aren't in real danger and you're getting familiar with what it feels like and looks like when "that man behind the curtain" is pulling the levers of your choices. This doesn't sound like much, but over time it's huge. You're leaving behind the tendency to react in ways that keep you defended but don't allow you to move forward.

How long or how often do you need to pause and notice? There are no rules. It's like stretching before you exercise— something your body needs more on some days and less on others.

Pausing to notice and soothe yourself is the vital but often missing step in leaving behind what is no longer serving you. When you welcome and soften at the edge of what's tolerable to you, you can more clearly see and gently detach from the dull, deadening side of *why bother* while patiently listening for what's calling you next. See which of the next sections strike a chord in you or make you flinch with a "not letting go of that" feeling. While you read, keep soothing your emotional immune system, so you can take in what I'm offering.

I'm Too Sad, Too Depressed, Too Anxious

Observing how you get in your own way can be a powerful behavior, a crucial first step toward leaving that behind, but if you're depressed, grieving, or anxious, it might not be possible or even a good idea. It can lead you deeper into rumination or lethargy, or you might find it impossible to be with yourself. You might find other moves more positive.

Because of my long history with depression, with a side helping of anxiety, and my years of grief, I have long been curious about what shifts our ability to engage in life. The cruelty of depression, anxiety, and grief is that the things that might make you feel better in the long term are often the most difficult to do in the moment. You know hanging out with people who love you is a good idea, but all you want to do is isolate and hunker under the covers with Netflix. You know aerobic exercise lifts your mood, but you can't drag yourself to go for a walk. As the belief that nothing can change sets in, you push yourself further into inaction. "What's the point?"

From 2001 to 2016, I lived on Bainbridge Island in Puget Sound, a ferry ride from Seattle. For a period of about a year, 2009 or 2010, I would drive my car onto the ferry deck, tuck myself in under my jacket, and after the ferry pulled away from the dock and got far enough into the shipping channel, I'd fantasize about jumping off. I'd imagine slipping over the rail so I could disappear and be done. That was my mantra: *done.*

Done feeling like I'd fucked up so much I was permanently fucked.

Done being exhausted by trying to be somebody better than I was: kinder, more patient, smarter, a better writer, a better parent.

Done second-guessing myself and hating myself for not knowing what I really wanted.

Done withholding myself from my new partner.

One early summer Saturday afternoon, waiting to drive onto the car deck, I watched tourists walking across the gangway onto the main deck, eating popcorn and herding children. A weekend summer ferry had a distinctly different feel from a weekday commuter ferry, more like a fair. On a clear day, the ride was a movie moment: downtown Seattle growing smaller as Mount Rainier popped into view, the iconic volcanic peak startling tourists and locals alike. Then you walked to the bow, and here came the Olympic Mountains, all craggy and snow-capped, with our tree-covered island nestled in front, complete with a picturesque harbor and rocky shores. You expected a soundtrack, folksy yet stirring. Fiddle, not cello.

After you drive onto the ferry, you have a choice: stay in your car or walk up two flights to the passenger deck, maybe buy a beer, visit with your neighbors, bitch about the downtown remodel. I hunkered down in my car. I wanted my fantasy. My partner, Bob, and I were fighting, which made me want to tell him he had to move out, a stupid overreaction, which made me want to run away from him even more. Lilly, my then fifteen-year-old daughter, was seriously depressed. She had contracted an antibiotic-resistant staph infection on her face from the artificial turf on the soccer field. Her once-perfect skin was crusty with what looked like acne but wasn't, her lymph nodes were constantly swollen and painful, and she was often exhausted. We'd been to the infectious disease specialist at the University of Washington and to alternative healers, she'd taken heavy-duty drugs, washed her face and body with a diluted bleach solution, but nothing worked. She had gone from being a confident kid to hiding at home when she wasn't in school. I was perennially guilty about my divorce from her dad two years earlier and for falling in love with Bob so soon after and blending our families sixteen months later. However much her mood was my fault or not, I was powerless to save her, which didn't stop me from trying—and then feeling even more powerless.

Then there was my work. After writing five successful books in eight years and being in demand as a speaker and teacher, I had written only one book in the last ten. It wasn't that I hadn't tried. I had one-and-a-half failed novels, half a dozen self-help book ideas, and half a memoir on my hard drive. I'd stopped emailing my agent to say, "I have a great new idea!" because I never followed up. The ideas all petered out and I didn't know why. When I tried to write, I had the recurring feeling that I was locked in an opaque glass room that was open at the top; if I could only scale the slick walls . . .

The ferry engines thrummed and we pulled away from the dock. I scanned the cars around me to see who else had stayed below. There was a dark-haired woman in a Volvo behind me, knitting. Two cars behind her an older couple shared a newspaper. Three cars ahead I could see a man's head and he appeared to be napping. That was it. Everybody else had gone upstairs. Perfect for me to play out my little narrative—if I wanted to jump, there were plenty of places where no one would see me go over the rail.

That's where my grim comfort ritual usually stopped. I didn't think about anything else except being *done*. But that day, maybe I was more depressed than usual, more worried about Lilly, more exhausted by the story line that I would always feel this stuck. More entrenched in the idea there was not a reason in the world to bother, because nothing would change. As I sat in my car, I imagined the short free fall after I let go of the ferry rail. My gasp as I plunged into the forty-nine-degree water—I had looked up the temperature. Sucking in the salty backlash of the ferry's wake as I surfaced. My heart would pound as cold-water shock set in. Without a life jacket, even in the summer, people sometimes died within minutes from the shock. If that didn't happen, you had about fifteen minutes, as your body drew your blood to your core and you lost the ability to swim. What would it be like to watch the ferry pull away while I paddled in place, my arms and legs growing heavier and heavier?

I shook my head. This was too real. *Stop.* What if Lilly or Bob or Aidan (Bob's son, now my bonus boy, the second child I had always wanted) or my mom ever knew I thought like this? What a shabby betrayal. I didn't want to die, not at all. There was so much about my life I cherished. I wasn't suffering from suicidal ideation; I was indulging in a self-pitying escape fantasy where I left all my shoulds and regrets in the car like old fast-food wrappers, stiff with dried grease. I should get off my ass and do something about being so stuck, take some of my advice—god knows I was full of it—but I didn't believe anything would work. I shifted in my seat, sighed. Maybe I should go upstairs and find someone to gossip with.

The PA system crackled. It startled me. Mid-trip announcements were unusual: an orca pod sighting (rare, as the pod was severely endangered, another depressing thought) or a family sprinkling someone's ashes (which really made me sad).

"Man overboard, man overboard!" The captain sounded as bewildered as I felt.

Reality tilted. Had someone heard my thoughts and busted me? *Forty-something self-pitying woman thinking about jumping off the car deck, all hands on deck.* The engines slowed and stopped.

"Crew, this is not a drill," came the voice again. "I repeat, this is not a drill. Begin emergency rescue." I opened my mouth to protest: "I was only fooling. I'd never really jump."

The woman in the Volvo behind me got out of her car to scan the water. Other people emerged from farther behind me and from the upper decks, clumped together at the rail. I opened my car door. The cold salty air focused me: this was real. Not a weird practical joke. Someone had gone overboard at the very moment I was thinking about jumping. The loudspeaker screeched and then the captain announced, "We have a woman overboard."

A woman. Holy shit. The captain paused and I looked around to see if anybody was glaring at me, sure I was somehow implicated. "This is not a drill," he continued, and then he took a breath and added, "Don't worry, we train for this."

Finally, after what seemed like hours, two crew members hurried by. Why weren't they running? I went right after them as if I were needed in the rescue. Two other crew members waited at the orange rescue Zodiac stored at the back of the ferry. How many times had I parked next to that raft but never considered what it was actually used for? Two of the crew got in, fussed with their life vests and the rescue ring. Once they were settled, the other men wrenched the raft over the railing and down the long white side of the ferry. "Hurry up," I wanted to scream. "Don't you know how cold that water is?"

Passengers hurried down one deck to the open back of the boat. I scurried after them. The water was choppy, the sun now hidden behind a scrim of blue clouds. We were in the middle of a busy shipping lane regularly crisscrossed by other passenger ferries, container ships stacked high, all sizes of sailboats, stalwart tugboats, fishing vessels, battleships, submarines, and cruise ships headed to Alaska.

I looked where other people were staring, but I couldn't see the woman. How far away would she be by now? I had no idea how fast the boat traveled, the physics of a moving object in water. "Did she fall off?" I asked the man in bike gear next to me.

Suddenly it was important to me that she fell.

"That would be pretty impossible," he said dryly, his cleats making a sound almost like tap shoes on the ferry deck. "The ferry has high railings for a reason."

"She jumped," I whispered. The Zodiac finally appeared around the stern and buzzed up the port side. It looked so small against all that water and sky. What was taking so long? I didn't think I'd asked this aloud until a man on my left said, "They have emergency training, but they aren't Navy SEALS. They're ferry workers."

I didn't answer. I was too busy thinking, "You really could die."

The stupidity of my fantasy had become the reality and it was the difference between watching a car accident on a TV show and watching one happen in front of you as you slam on the brakes. When Lilly was sixteen, we went skydiving for her birthday. Both of us were as calm as if we were going to the movies. I jumped first, strapped to a burly, bearded instructor who wore too much aftershave. The free fall snatched the air from my lungs, and as I hurtled toward the ground all I could think was "Lilly will hate this!" I willed myself to reverse, like a cartoon character, and fly back into the opening of the rickety plane and grab her before she jumped. But all I could do was keep falling. I hated the whole descent even after I, and then Lilly, landed safely. If it had been me in the icy water, that's what I imagined I would feel. *Go back!* Go back to my Bob and his ginger beard tickling my face when he kissed me good morning and told me, "Baby, I love you so much." Go back to the kids sleepily negotiating who took a shower first, go back to one dog curled next to my belly and the other at the back of my knees, go back to sitting at my desk wondering what I might create next. *Go back!*

The Zodiac slowed to a stop maybe half a mile behind us. We could see the men pulling someone aboard, but they were so tiny that it was hard to see. I shivered. I kept my eye on the raft as they executed a wide turn and came back. I had to witness this freaky coincidence completely, burn it into my head.

I ran back up to where the boat was being hauled up. I stared as she rose up, displayed on a neon-orange platter. There was something about her body language that pissed me off. She laid across the back pontoon with her arm thrown across her face like she was in a play, like the whole event had been staged. She wore a flowered dress and sandals, and her skin was blue-white. I looked to be sure her chest was moving.

One of the crew barked, "You people, move away. Let this woman have some space." I stumbled back, mortified to have been caught gaping. Yet I lingered. I couldn't take my eyes off her. "Move on," the man growled again. The spell broken, I scurried back to my car, my head down.

I grabbed my jacket from the back seat. My teeth were clacking together, but my face burned with shame. Why had she jumped? Did she think her life had passed her by, that she couldn't make a new one? Was she imagining the relief of being done, no longer trying to make her life as good as she taught other women it could be? Was she pissed they rescued her? Or stupefied with gratitude? Had she planned it or simply found herself at the railing and then *plop!* over? Why had her life become something she didn't want to bother about?

The engines shifted into gear and the ferry lumbered toward Eagle Harbor. I rocked back and forth to calm myself enough to think, to make sense of the coincidence.

Now, if this were a movie, my life would have turned around right then and there, my regrets and lingering depression blasted away by gratitude. Colors would have been brighter, food more delicious, every encounter with another human luminous with love. Instead, I was ashamed and embarrassed. I felt bitch-slapped by a cosmic trickster. I told no one what happened, not for years. That's one way that depression replicates itself, by convincing us to personalize everything.

When I was depressed and grieving, and I found these lines from a Rumi poem, I was startled into considering freedom: "Out beyond ideas of rightdoing and wrongdoing, there is a field. / I will meet you there." I had felt fenced in with high walls of razor wire and guarded by fierce men in armed towers—and at the same time, I was living in a vaster world, fresh and unfettered, free of my endless self-judgment and shoulda woulda couldas. Here's what was so astonishing to me: these two states coexisted! Instead of believing I had to feel better before I engaged with life again, I could let myself be as I was *while* opening to feeling alive again.

Depression, sadness, and anxiety can have complex causes and many mitigating factors. Our genetic makeup, trauma, what we eat and drink all impact our mood. Sugar is not my mood's friend and, sadly, neither is wine. Culture plays a role too, much bigger than is often acknowledged. Imagine if when you were grieving or depressed, your whole community gathered to grieve with you or to dance with you or to listen to you? And imagine a community in which feeling what you are feeling was accepted and celebrated, instead of judged or wished away? And imagine if you had access to the resources you need to flourish?

These factors influence us and yet there is always room, even if only a tiny wiggly bit of room on a very bad day, to venture out into the field beyond rightdoing and wrongdoing. The path into the field is made of supreme self-kindness.

Our hearts grow weary when we are depressed and grieving, and that weariness can become a hardness, a defense against being hurt again. Bothering again, even a tiny bit, motivated me to do the things I needed to do to repair my brain and spirit, like practicing yoga, staying away from sugar, getting aerobic exercise, and going back to therapy. When I kept waiting to know why things had gone south and exactly what would make me care again, I only sank deeper into my gloom.

Maybe you need time to grieve. Dana told me that after a personal and professional betrayal, she gave herself "two months to lie on the couch and cry and surrender to my sadness, and make that the only thing I was doing. It was the single most self-loving thing I have ever done. I think if I had tried to bury my feelings and move on, I would not be feeling

"Life is waiting for you. You might be stuck here for a while, but the world isn't going anywhere. Hang on in there if you can. Life is always worth it."

MATT HAIG, REASONS TO STAY ALIVE

as strong and happy as I do now. I would not be getting to the light side of *why bother.*" After Dana gave herself the time to grieve, she volunteered at a local organic farm and connected deeply with nature, finding in that humble relationship a healthy way to let go of her big dream and find her next *why bother.* "I will bother because I can. Because life is a gift. Because I am a creative being. Because there is meaning to be found by showing up again and again to answer the question in ways large and small, and in the most intimate, personal ways that only each individual can."

Depression and other mental illnesses are conditions we learn to work with by finding the therapists, medications, and other approaches that suit us, refusing, as Jennee told me about living with bipolar disorder, "to let it define me any longer." What causes and what helps us with a mood disorder is still very much a mystery—we don't yet know enough about the brain. That alone can make you shrug "Why bother?" but there can also be, on a good day, a sense of creative power in knowing you are the expert on you and your experiments matter and can make a difference. Nobody but me could have discovered that running improved my mood or that even a little sugar sends me spiraling down. I do know it's helpful to leave behind, as you are able, the story of "you can't" because you are too old or too young or too whatever. I could not have gotten my bother on if I had stayed in my old stories. Meet me in the field beyond rightdoing and wrongdoing. I found freedom and hope there and perhaps you can too.

I Don't Have the Energy

Whatever your mood and physical state, there's a component of deciding what to leave behind that many of my readers have found indispensable. I call it minimum requirements for self-care. The idea is simple: there are basic things you need in place to pursue a fulfilling life. Without these basics, it's far easier to fall into and stay stuck in the yuck kind of *why bother*.

But here's the critical bit: we're terrible at paying attention to these basics, so they easily fall by the wayside and then wreak havoc in our lives, sometimes creating a feeling of lassitude and pointlessness all by themselves. We become so accustomed to doing without or feeling like crap, we give up, and that giving up spreads to our whole life. I've seen people who start to pay decent attention to these minimums lift themselves out of the murk of "Who cares about anything?" and that alone turns their blah into shine.

What are these basics? Here are some from my students: plenty of sleep, solitude, reading for pleasure, cuddling and playing with pets, morning prayers, long walks, journaling, time to create, nature, silence, sex, hugs or other touch, meditation, laughing with friends, volunteering, recovery meetings, baths, and being near or in water. You don't do all your minimums every day (or there would be no time to work, let alone eat) or even every week, but do enough so you have what you need for a solid foundation of health, well-being, energy, and contact with yourself. Life will never be perfect, but it also shouldn't always be a constant deficit. If it is, you may well be looking at the very things you must leave behind to bother again.

Life is challenging, whether you're caring for a child with special needs or a parent with dementia or living from paycheck to paycheck or trying to get your first job without any experience in your field and a mountain of student debt. And I've seen too many people refuse to make changes that would help them meet their minimums more often. Jackie offered elaborate excuses as to why her partner couldn't help with childcare and housework. Every day Pat visited her father in memory care even when he no longer recognized her and slept through most of her visits and the forty-minute drive each way consumed all the time she had for self-care and her writing. Marlene refused to join the local hiking club because she was "out of shape" even though there were plenty of easy hikes scheduled, and she was afraid of going for hikes by herself, so she stopped getting outside and exercising altogether.

Take out a journal or scrap of paper and make a list of what you need to feel like yourself and to have sufficient energy to bother again. Pay close attention to the things you don't think are worth writing down because "nothing could ever change" or because something (or someone else) has to change first. These will not be exciting or sexy. They will probably be garden variety, even boring. But each has the potential to give you a crucial boost. These are not goals or resolutions, but *why bother* canaries. You know how miners carried canaries into the coal mines and if the canaries died, the miners knew to get out fast? This list is your canary.

Check your list frequently and ask yourself, "When is the last time I...?" Watch out for your emotional immune system pulling the curtain over your need for more rest or alone time by insisting things are fine as they are. It's weird that we do that to ourselves. You would think you would easily give yourself what you need, but even the most basic kind of self-care can bring up feelings of self-ishness, vulnerability, even a mistrust of pleasure. Plus, when our nervous system has been jacked up, it's hard to make the switch from hustling to being with yourself. Circle back to your list, and practice pausing if you notice you're denying yourself minimum requirements. Or start small with one thing that gives you real pleasure. This is not about self-improvement; this is about sweet, steady self-support.

To read about other people's minimum requirements and get regular reminders to check in with yours, go to jenniferlouden.com/whybother.

For bonus points, share your list with someone you trust and ask them what's missing or what you haven't made time for recently (or in forever). And then support them to make a list too.

I'm Too Old and It's Too Late

But what exactly are you too old for? And how are you determining it's too late?

Yes, you are too old for some activities and pursuits that once lit you up or that you envisioned being part of your life. But the quip "Been there, done that" is actually a blessing and ground to stand on. You've lived a thousand lifetimes already. You have collected an encyclopedia of experiences with sweat and tears. Thankfully, your personal research library is invaluable in this betwixt-between place.

Physical pain, insomnia, and the steady absence of those who have died are very real but why are they—or whatever else is happening—a reason to stop living? Why are any of the experiences, losses, and triumphs tattooed on your heart a reason to halt your becoming? We are always becoming, and that never ends, not until our last breath—and then who knows, maybe it continues. We'll find out.

Around the time of the ferry incident, when I was sure I would spend the rest of my life doing nothing worthwhile or compelling, my friend Michael called to chat. I was sitting on the front porch trying to motivate myself to do something with my day when Lilly brought me the phone.

I tried to fake a happy mood.

"You don't sound great," Michael said.

I shifted my chair so my legs would be in the sun. It was one of those Pacific Northwest summer days that made living through the rainy winters worth it.

"I'm just in a midlife funk," I said. The twins from down the street rode their bikes past me. They'd stuck playing cards in their bike spokes, and the thwacking sound reminded me of being a kid, when summer was forever. That made me even more sad. I would never feel that spaciousness again.

"What part of midlife's got you down?" Michael asked.

"The part about it being too late and me being too old. A few weeks ago, my high school hosted a reunion, some mid-decade thing where they invited different years to return together. My cousin went, and she emailed me about it. Somebody had the bright idea to print out what people wrote in the yearbook about what we'd accomplish in the ten years after high school and tie the cards to balloons. One balloon kept hitting my cousin in the head, so she grabbed it and read the card. It was mine, what I wrote in the yearbook. She was so embarrassed by the cocky tone of what I wrote, she hid the balloon under the table for the rest of the night."

"What did you say that was so bad? That you wanted to rule the world?"

"I don't even want to tell you."

"You know you do."

I recited it in a monotone as if these weren't once my deepest dreams: "Write two-and-a-half novels, write and direct three movies, win an Oscar, have one-and-a-half children, and split my time between Switzerland and New York." I pretended to laugh at myself. "Remember I was going to do that all in ten years."

"One of the best
guides to how to
be self-loving is to
give ourselves
the love we are often
dreaming about
receiving
from others."

———————

BELL HOOKS,
ALL ABOUT LOVE

Michael laughed. "That half-child might be difficult to find clothes for." I laughed for real, and a little of my mortification eased. "It's a good thing your cousin hid that balloon," he added.

"She must have picked up I was all about wanting to be special. I remember writing that blurb, thinking I would show everybody." I studied my toes. I needed a pedicure. "But a part of me thought I could. That I would."

"I know what you mean," Michael said. "I was a Rhodes scholar, and some people I was at Oxford with—one guy's a big city mayor and no doubt will end up running for president, and people won Genius Grants, and somebody's a billionaire. Bloody hell. I regularly go, 'WTF?'" I took the phone away from my ear and stared at it. Michael was the most confident person I knew. Secure in his abilities and his intellect, founder of a multi-million-dollar training company, he was my gold standard for confidence and success. "But you can't feel that way. You're the *man*."

Michael snorted. "I reckon we all do."

That summer day, my friend pricked a hole in my story of "I'm too old and it's too late." He reminded me it's not unique to feel disappointment about our lives; it's inevitable. When we're young, we don't understand what life will throw at us, both beautiful and terrible. It's impossible to live the story you imagine at twenty or forty. Deciding you can't bother because your story didn't unfold the way you thought it would, or should, is self-cruelty of the highest degree. It's declaring,

"Because my life doesn't look the way I think it should, I give up." Or "Because I can't do or have this particular thing, my life has no meaning."

Doesn't that strike you as mercilessly narrow and harsh?

When you get down to it, we all long to live the fullest life we can and to love honestly. And we all desire to leave the world a slightly better place by our presence and actions. That's where desire ultimately leads us. Where does that put me in relationship to the woman on the porch bemoaning all she didn't do? What would I tell her now? "You did what many people do. You confused what you've accomplished for how well you've lived. You believed creating mattered only if it got you a movie deal or a bestselling novel and with it, a pretty life. But all along, you were figuring out how to live. Now you know: creating matters, in all forms, because it calls you to life. And now you know that loving well, people and planet, is your greatest desire."

In his book *Beauty*, John O'Donohue writes, "Of the many callings in the world, the invitation to the adventure of an awakened and full life is the most exhilarating." Tell me: how can you ever be too old or too far behind, how can it ever be too late, for that?

I'm Too Broke

I have a fraught relationship with money. I inherited my dad's fear of not having enough to keep myself and those I love safe. In addition, for years, I mangled my creative desires because I was too consumed with how much money I made from them. It caused a torturous split in me: part of me was so devoted to truth and service and creative expression and another to safety and prestige. Each time I found myself needing to rediscover my relationship to desire and perhaps do something different, my fears about money added a layer of confusion and gut-twisting and caused me not to listen. In one *why bother* period in my mid-thirties, I convinced myself I wanted my comfortable house more than I wanted to rediscover my mojo. I turned away from even entertaining the question.

I'm not beating myself up for those choices—pursuing opportunities for financial security allowed me to make enough money to support my daughter, to make sure she had a good education and a safe place to live. I was able to pay for my health care as a self-employed writer and I saved money for retirement. This all makes me proud and lucky. Yet I can't help but wonder how much I exaggerated my money needs and fears, and sometimes still do. I assumed that any change I might make meant certain permanent poverty, and I never truly tested that assumption. I never went all in on writing fiction or teaching yoga and meditation, for example. Not that those would have necessarily been better choices for me, but not allowing myself to explore them added to my personal *why bother* deficit.

When Robin wrote me about retiring from her job as a high school drama teacher and her plan to become a nomad, I felt her courage and excitement. Robin wrote, "One evening a year ago, I sat on my porch and I received an answer to the prayer I had been reciting. *You will have to give up some of what you love if you want to find what will make you grow again.*" Robin was praying because she was deeply depressed and felt all the best parts of her life were over and "all I had to look forward to was decay, diminishment, and death. My mom was deteriorating mentally and physically in an assisted living facility. My four adult children were spread throughout the country. My job as a high school drama teacher was no longer my passion or purpose. What was I going to do with the next twenty-five years?"

Then Robin slipped on water in the school hallway, shattering her kneecap and dislocating her leg. After four months of rehab, she emerged "free and grateful and awake" and decided to heed the answer to her prayer. She retired early. She's worried, of course, that she will end up lonely and poor, but she also said, "I get to find out who I am now, what I love, and what I desire. I had forgotten what joy and wonder felt like. Now life is not something to just get through but to engage with again. I feel something I haven't felt in years. I feel hope and love. I think this change is the biggest and best mistake I have ever made."

Do you have to throw everything out the window and give up financial security to find your *what's next*? Or do you have to get out of debt, find a better job, save enough for a down payment on a house before you can bother? You won't know the answer until you engage with the question, "What cost am I willing to pay for a life that I want to bother about?"

Follow-up questions might include:

- Where am I assuming I don't have a choice?
- Where am I choosing comfort over aliveness?
- Who or what is blocking me from having more choice?

We live in an unjust world. In the US, for example, 0.1 percent of the population makes 188 times as much as the bottom 90 percent. Social support systems in most countries have been sold out from under us. One in five Americans forgo health care because they can't afford it—even *with* health insurance. It takes a Black woman, on average, twenty months to earn what a white man can earn in twelve. For Latinx or Indigenous women, the numbers skew even worse. But will we take action against those inequalities if we aren't connected to what we care about? We don't want to put the blame for systemic inequality on our shoulders—the system loves when we do that—but we also don't want to allow the system to trap us into thinking there is nothing we can do, or to settle for numbing out.

One of my aunts embezzled $40,000. What did she buy with the money? Mostly exotic birds. A whole roomful. I looked at my aunt—undereducated, bored, lonely, trapped in a tiny town—and I see someone who lacked the opportunity to make a more fulfilling life. How much choice did she have to find another way to bother? I'm not letting her off the hook for her poor choices, but I also refuse to ignore the larger context of what was available to her.

We will bother about the strangest things and in the most destructive ways if we aren't able to make a life of purpose and connection. We can't ignore money; we can't wish it away or repeat prosperity affirmations until we pass out. We can recognize that the system is rigged for the benefit of the few and that the dominant story of "more stuff = more status and happiness" is an elaborate con. Oh yes, we want *more*, but not more money: more pleasure, more joy, more love, more creativity, more peace, more justice, more life. Yes, we work to elect representatives who will reform the system; yes, we can search for and create ways to take care of ourselves that are more community based and less transactional; yes, we can learn about how money works and get out of credit card debt. But let's do it with the sly grin of the coyote rather than with gritted teeth, steely determination, fear, and shame.

Money will influence, shape, prevent, and enable how you bother. You will be free as long as you refuse to use lack of money as an excuse to shut down your desire, as long as you refuse to buy the story that you are separate from life itself or that you have to purchase the willingness to bother. Nurture that freedom.

I'm Too Ill

Illness presents special challenges to finding the desire to discover what's next. Being sick takes all your focus and energy and can be a full-time job.

I have never been ill like my friend Oriah, who has spent thirty-eight years living with an autoimmune disorder that makes getting out of bed some days almost impossible, or like my friend June, who was in a terrible car accident as a young woman and has dealt with chronic pain and hepatitis C ever since. But I have spent a big chunk of my life feeling half ill, probably because of a childhood accident. Even as I write this, I notice a pressure in my sinuses, a light fatigue, a touch of nausea. I have felt far, far worse—fatigue so bad I would worry before I taught a retreat or gave a speech that I would have to quit halfway through. I look back on most of Lilly's life and see myself lying on the couch, watching her play or fobbing her off on friends. I found ways to manage my symptoms, including several surgeries, and I've mostly made my peace with rarely feeling 100 percent rested, energetic, and clear-headed. I don't want to define myself as someone who's sick, and frankly, I used to use feeling sick as an excuse to hide from myself and life.

I also experienced a seven-year mysterious back aliment where my muscles twisted so severely my physical therapist said, "I would think you had scoliosis if I didn't know better." As with my general fatigue and yuckiness, I tried everything for my back. I started with mainstream stuff like physical therapy, but as the years and pain piled on, the treatments got wackier, all my extra money going to pay for whatever new treatment I heard about. Fascial counterstrain; energy healing in many forms; physical therapy with a young woman who inserted her finger in my vagina to release my overly enthusiastic pelvic floor; a complicated deep-tissue massage and weight training program that including wearing a lift in my shoe and sitting on the edge of a rubber cushion at my desk, one cheek off, one cheek on; hot yoga; asking my body in my journal, "Body, what do you need to tell me to heal?"; Pilates; neck traction; medical intuitive. What finally worked? I moved to Colorado and my friend Mel told me about her physical therapist. Charlie fixed my back in three weeks with a combination of dry needling, massage, adjustments, and his attitude, which made me believe I was normal and completely healable.

Most of my back pain happened during my worst *why bother* time and while I suspect the two were related, it doesn't matter. My back pain wasn't a punishment for what was happening, and I wish I could have realized that sooner. I spent so much time panicking and pushing myself to get better. I was ashamed for not healing—and several health care providers shamed me for not getting well. I wonder if trusting myself that I was doing the best I knew how at the time might have helped. Because bothering was happening for me big time—I cared fiercely about getting better. This truth got lost in the struggle and boredom of trying to get well, buried under the fear of never getting my life back.

There's a lot in life that never has a point, and I, for one, am heartily sick of being told when I've suffered that "what doesn't kill you makes you stronger." I swear the only people who say that have not really suffered.

Appreciating that you know how to care for your life force by assisting your healing? That's different. Your *why bother* instinct is working. There is no point in judging this kind of bothering as less than another kind. It's possible that your work on healing is strengthening your ability to bother in ways that may surprise you—and yes, that's a bit of "there's a gift in this crap," so take that with a grain of salt. But illness, like grief, teaches a form of fierce discernment.

Sometimes, giving yourself full permission to focus on nothing but healing can be a great relief. Let the rest of the world carry on; you'll be back when you're ready. Other times, you need something else going on or you'll feel too isolated and hopeless. That's when the concept of a human-scaled life can be useful. Our culture hammers us, healthy or sick, with the idea we should be superhuman. Superhuman in our productivity, our health, our creativity, our looks, how much we earn—you name it, we should do more. There is always another article or another expert telling you how to hack the system, win the prize, get ahead. Those articles and experts so rarely mention the wealth or pay gap, your company demanding you to do the equivalent of three jobs, the expectation that you answer messages and emails at all hours and on weekends. The message is insidious and ever-present: being a human, let alone a sick human, is never enough.

What I preach is to work within your limits and use them to be more creative. When you have to work three jobs to pay the rent or your boss messages you to tell you to get on a plane and all you want to do is sleep, I know my idea of a human-scaled life is laughable. You're trying to survive. But even when we can't escape what's required of us, we can reframe what else we insist we should be doing. Especially if we are ill.

Working within your limits is understanding that you're capable of far more than you can imagine, while realizing you need to choose wisely given the reality you're living. What I would do instead of embracing my low-grade icky feeling or my back twisty-ness was collapse and throw myself a pity party, complete with either too much wine or sugar, or I would decide I was fine, good to go, push myself, and then get worse. Neither of these choices freed me to bother again nor to get well. By accepting that I was a "fragile flower," as one friend lovingly labeled me, I started to plan my days and my self-care with more care and discernment. I let go of how I should be and embraced how I was—without giving up. All the talk of limitless possibilities that I picked up from the New Age culture and the life hacks from the tech world did nothing but mess with my head. But so did thinking I couldn't bother again because I was too sick.

For many years, Wendy and her husband had worked toward moving to Nepal. Her husband's role as a doctor at a large teaching hospital there was clear. It took Wendy more time to work out how to be useful. After a few months living there, she was invited to teach jewelry making and to mentor a local project that helped abused women earn sustainable incomes. She loved it and things were going well. Six months later, when they briefly returned to Australia to settle a visa issue, Wendy became seriously ill. "I was hospitalized for eight weeks and the likelihood of us ever returning to Nepal pretty much vanished. The move to Nepal was my shot at deep happiness, at living my dream! We had worked so hard, sacrificed so much, left behind so much to get there. There was no plan B. I couldn't truly be happy anywhere else. If that was the case, why bother? I remember lying in bed, thinking, 'Okay. We'll probably never go back. So I have to learn to find happiness that doesn't depend on that. To learn to go with change rather than fighting it, because otherwise I have might have lots of sad years ahead of me.' I started to learn how to bother but not by fanatically controlling my life. I realized that simply being alive and waking up healthy was enough of a reason to bother, and that bothering meant something quite different to what I had thought."

Being ill might well reshape how you bother and what you bother about, but illness has taught me that bothering is possible no matter what. It's taught me it isn't all my fault and that I only have so much control. It's taught me to stop looking for a magic solution or for someone to rescue me. It's taught me to measure what I do rather than what I didn't do or wish I had done. It's taught me when I do have energy or feel well, to go fully after what I want to bother about even if I have no idea what it means or where it will lead. For that, I am begrudgingly grateful.

I Never Get a Break

Not all of us have the power or latitude to easily re-create our lives, our career paths, or our relationships—in fact, most of us don't. We need the paycheck; we work in fields or situations that restrict our autonomy, our creativity, even our values. And we have families, partners, neighbors, and environments that are draining and toxic. A child addicted to drugs, an emotionally withdrawn partner, an unresponsive landlord, long and stressful commutes, micro and macro aggressions, expensive day care...

What do you do when faced with a situation you can't readily change or leave? How do you know where to start? For now, consider how the natural creative process of bothering can enliven you. This may seem feeble in the face of your male colleague earning more than you or your kid disappearing into the streets again, but still, I ask you to consider it. What I did not understand for an embarrassingly long time is the *why bother* juncture requires us to reorient to life in a

new way. *You cannot go back to life as usual.* You can't insist
you get the life you wanted rather than the life you now have.
Well, you can keep insisting, but it takes so much energy. Lord
knows I exhausted myself this way, craving the comfort of the
past, the ways things had been, the way they were *supposed* to
be, the way I wanted them to be, even as it dragged me down
into lifelessness.

It never occurred to me that what was happening was as
familiar as the veins on the back of my hands: the creative
process writ large, the creative process of life itself. Life asking me to live again. Creativity as a method rather than as a
product.

When I first realized *why bother* was actually a fertile and
vital place to be instead of zombie land (let me be clear, I
would realize this for about ten seconds at a time and then
go back to grinding my teeth and trying to do the same old,
same old), I thought, "How ironic!" Ironic because I've spent
most of my life creating stuff. Creating makes life meaningful
for me. But somewhere along the way, I turned the creative
process into a product, into an identity, into a way to prove
myself worthy, to gain love and approval, to get to where I
would finally be good enough. I messed with being creative
for so long I no longer recognized it.

Maybe we all do this, in different ways: mess with the natural cycle of creating what we want. There are probably ten
million Instagram posts encouraging us to let go, trust life,
that everything will take care of itself. Those posts irritate

"In my way of thinking, anything is possible. Life is at the bottom of things and belief at the top, while the creative impulse, dwelling in the center, informs all."

PATTI SMITH, M TRAIN

the hell out of me. They make bothering again seem like a switch you can throw or something pretty you can buy and *bam!* all is juicy, compelling, and fulfilling again. Or maybe, just maybe, I hate them because I complicated my *why bother* passages, and thus prolonged them. For *years*, I put my attention on *I can't, I won't, it's not possible* instead of on *I want, I might, I wonder.*

Whatever you think of the natural creative process idea, you must take back your energy from trying to land your ideal job or save your child or find a loving partner. Take your energy back from worrying, complaining, and trying to change others, and turn your attention toward what is good, what is beckoning. Nurture the connection to goodness and life, which flows to you no matter what. Wrench your focus away from what is wrong and heartbreaking, and stop trying to solve things. I'm not placing all the responsibility on you or ignoring the environment that influences you. I'm suggesting that filling yourself up with life will make it more possible to work for meaningful change. Why bother to keep trying to do what you can't possibly do—yet?

Kelly wrote me soon after her brother died. She was experiencing bouts of unemployment and had suffered through numerous family tragedies. She was twenty-nine years sober "and still doing the world one day at a time. A part of me lost the magic and another part is cynical about most spiritual things I see in the world, but there is still something deep inside whispering. For now, I'll call it a Knowing." She trusted what she had when she was getting sober: her heart. "As long as it was beating, I knew there was still hope. As long as my heart was beating, I still had a chance and a choice. As long as there's a beat and breath, I'll continue to bother."

Your work situation or your family or your loneliness or your recovery may be very painful. You do not deny this by taking a break. You acknowledge that you can't do anything about it right now and you need to get your life force back, so you can collaborate in making a fulfilling life for yourself. You're gathering the energy and clarity to decide what to change or how you can make your peace with the situation; you are not giving up and you are not placing the responsibility solely on your own shoulders. You are welcoming *what's next* into your life.

I'm Not Good Enough

Can you imagine how much easier it would be to bother about whatever the hell you wanted if we all blew up the deadening, dulling worry of not being good enough once and for all? Can you imagine how much energy, leadership, power, and innovation we would release? What a full-throttle roar of "Why the hell not!" would reverberate around the earth?

When I look back at all the ways I have let "I'm not good enough" limit me, I burn with rage that I ever bought the bullshit cultural story that in order to matter, I had to be better than I am. Because that's what the insidious, hideous story that not being good enough teaches us: we shouldn't bother because we don't deserve to, unless we fit certain parameters.

When we believe we aren't good enough, when we think stretching to do our best is the same as proving our worth, we can't relax into life and let it reveal the marvels that await. We're too busy checking out how we compare to everybody else, worrying we're about to be busted as an imposter, or trying to perfect our every effort.

Please consider that any thoughts you have of not being enough aren't factual and are *not* personal. I like to frame these thoughts as alien invaders because it reminds me my feelings of not-enoughness are not organic to me but created by a culture that thrives on making people, especially women, people of color, differently abled people, and LGBTQ folks, feel less than. Then I remember to wonder: "Why does that alien invader exist? What purpose does it serve? Who benefits?" Perhaps its purpose is to distract us and keep us from noticing how many of us don't have equal rights, equal pay, or equal power. When we believe the earworm of "not good enough," we take part in the systems that oppress us, which is an elegant mindfuck indeed. We incessantly focus on our flaws rather than on the enormous flaws in the system.

Feeling not good enough isn't only a societal construct. Some of those feelings persist because of our childhood experiences, trauma's aftereffects, or the way our brains normally function. And while exploring various means of healing can be beneficial, we can, in some respects, take a similar approach to these sources of insufficiency: we can question their validity.

Try listening to yourself first, and other people and "experts" second. When you catch yourself comparing yourself to others or you feel like a fake, consider this to be the burbling of subjectivity and culture versus the Truth. Gently question all the ways you have been taught to self-police, whether that is your anger, your excitement, your curiosity, your lust for life, or how you look.

In the end, not feeling good enough determines nothing. It has no real power to block you from whatever it is you'll discover as you move through this process that brings you to life. If it did, I would still be sitting on the ferry thinking about how good it would feel to slip over the edge and be done. You don't have to get over anything to get on with life. Hold your story with love, look for the facts, notice how not being good enough comes from the culture instead of automatically believing its unicorn tales that's it is in you. Since you do not know what will show up for you to care about next or how it will unfold, any thoughts of not being good enough are beside the point.

But then they always were.

I've put together more help to banish feelings of not being good enough at jenniferlouden.com/whybother.

I Don't Want to Let Go of Who I Am

You don't know who or what will show up as you leave behind
what you no longer bother about and venture into new territory. By that I don't mean other people but rather the who that
you will become. You will refresh and rearrange how you see
yourself as you venture through this passage, and that entails
leaving behind some of the ways you see yourself now.

I was talking to a coaching client, Aliyah, about her desire
to write. She's fifty-six, the president of a successful family
company, and almost ready to retire. "I didn't choose my
career," she said. "It's not the work or the industry I would
have ever chosen for myself, but my family needed me, so I
stepped in. I'm very, very good at what I do. Now I'm thinking
about doing other things, like writing, that I choose to do but
I'm not very good at." She was quiet for a long moment. "I
don't know if I can be devoted to something I'm not good at."

I could feel Aliyah peering over the edge from how she had
defined herself for the last twenty-eight years, feeling into
what it would be like to let go of her image: someone who did
everything well and did what was expected of her, someone
whom everybody counted on. "In this next phase of your life,"
I said, "you decide if something's worth it. Nobody else." Aliyah stared at me unblinkingly and then slowly nodded.

On a run after our session, I reflected on how Aliyah recognized that she had to let go of what she had been or she
would end up constructing a similar life for herself after she

retired. I was confident she was up for learning a new way of caring, one that wasn't based on her old identity or confined by mastery or defined by pleasing her family. Just because something changes in your life—retirement, career, the death of a spouse, recovery from cancer, moving to a new state or country—doesn't guarantee you'll be open to what's next. Sometimes we can't give up who we've been, even if outer circumstances change or our life is boring, unsatisfying, a half-life. Staying attached to our old identities is a common way to shove ourselves into not bothering, and we are usually blind to how holding on is causing the block.

It's sometimes harder for men to let go of the story that who they've been defines them in some essential way. Mark spent most of his adult life working for a well-known educational nonprofit. "I could never adequately explain to people what I did, but all I had to do was mention who I worked for and everybody was in awe. When the funding got cut for my project and, after a period of unemployment, I went to work for an obscure organization nobody ever heard of, I was astonished at how freaked out I was. I thought once I had a job again, I would calm down but no. I had to peel off my identity as 'powerful and connected' first."

When you are on the other side and bothering again, you'll look back and think, "What was I so freaked out about?" But before? It can feel like dying. In a way, you *are* dying. To find *what's next*, you must allow your old self to die and write a new story of what matters to you now. It sounds awfully trite, but this excruciating inner work almost always takes more time and energy than we imagine it will. That can feel so frustrating given we live in a culture where crafting a new identity seems like it should be as quick and easy as dyeing your hair, whitening your teeth, and getting a little Botox. Thank god it's not that easy, because doing the patient inner work of shifting your self-concept creates the container for your new life. I know because, like all of us, I have had to let go of who I wanted to be many times. Here's a story of the first time.

It's the late summer of 1987. I'm twenty-five. I've been out of film school for a year and a few months. My entire reason for being is to make it as a very successful screenwriter, preferably before the year is over.

I have a halfway decent agent, I've had a handful of meetings with development executives, and I'm working on a new screenplay. By all rights, I should be hopeful. Only I'm not. I'm depressed, I'm drinking too much red wine at night, and I'm utterly stuck.

I sit at my kitchen table in a tiny, rented guesthouse, staring at my computer screen, rewriting the same four or five pages. My memory of those hot smoggy months is of a blinking cursor, three young women characters who refused to come alive, and then, at some point, an inner voice whispering I needed to try something else for a little while. I remember the warm appeal as I considered giving up the fight to be a writer and then my icy horror. I couldn't stop writing. I needed to become a successful writer. A Somebody. And quickly.

The inner voice didn't go away. In fact, it got louder as it tried to get my attention and wake me up. In my favorite bookstore, it would insist I look for Help Wanted signs. Driving by the garden store, it would nag me about how much I loved gardening; why not explore that interest, get an entry-level job? When I was in step aerobics, it would chant along with the beat of "Walk Like an Egyptian"—"You could lead this class"—which was absurd given I stepped left when the rest of the class stepped right. But the voice kept nattering and prodding.

The voice began to editorialize more: "You need to be kinder to yourself. You need to quit writing." This advice made me want to find an exorcist. It was one thing to suggest another job as a way to make some money (which was necessary, since I'd quit my job as a reader at a big Hollywood talent agency, certain I would soon sell my screenplay for half a million dollars), but it was quite another thing to ask me to quit writing. If I gave up my dream, I was certain I would die. Die as in I couldn't see anything else for me beyond writing and successfully selling this screenplay. The world was flat and I would fall off. I *had* to become a successful screenwriter.

When did I finally surrender to the inner prompting to take a break, to ease up, to try something else? Perhaps I had a wine hangover or perhaps I was tired of lying to myself about my agent "waiting" for my screenplay when I knew he probably didn't even remember I was his client. Or perhaps I'd had enough of kicking myself for not being who I wanted to be.

For whatever combination of reasons, I decided to take a break. And to make it real, the part of me that enjoyed

self-torture called my friend Nicole. She'd decided to be
a writer a year and a half earlier, on a whim. She'd already
secured a better agent than mine and optioned a screenplay
idea for actual money. Yes, I was envious of Nicole. But the real
source of my envy? Nicole loved to write. She wrote all the time.

"Hello," Nicole answered. She'd acquired a faint English
accent on a recent trip to London. I rolled my eyes.

There was no time for niceties. "I'm quitting writing," I
blurted out. There, I'd said it. I put my hand on my chest to
see if I still existed. I tried to take a deep breath, but I couldn't.
I was invisible and dying.

"If that's what you want," Nicole said, sounding bored.

"Maybe just for a month," I almost whispered as the room
telescoped like the film shot Alfred Hitchcock had invented
and I had mimicked in several of my student films. I gripped
the kitchen counter to stay upright. "I need a break," I added,
more to myself than Nicole. She changed the subject, talked
about how her writing was going fabulously well. I pressed the
receiver hard against my ear. I was dissolving.

I hung up, knowing I had made a terrible mistake. Who the
fuck cared what my inner voice said? I'd write again tomorrow. I'd try a new story, a fresh idea. I tried to fight my way
back to "being a screenwriter," to convince myself tomorrow
would be different.

But I found I could not. I had no fight left in me.

Standing by the kitchen counter, I did the only thing I
could: I surrendered being a writer.

I've tried to understand for thirty years what happened next. *Free fall* is the best I've come up with, only it wasn't frightening. Not at all. I was lightness itself, falling and rising at the same time. The leaden weight of trying so hard to become somebody, to prove I was special, floated off me. For the first time since I had moved to L.A. six years before to "make it" in the film business, I was okay. Simply okay.

After a time, maybe two minutes or maybe half an hour, still rooted to the same spot, I heard a voice very clearly say, "The Woman's Comfort Book." I turned to see if my landlord, who lived right above me, had stuck her head in my apartment and spoken to me. But there was no one there.

That title eventually became a bestselling book and launched my career. But this is not a story about getting what you want; this is a story about the gateway of letting go. Because, ironically, letting go of my story that I had to become a successful screenwriter to matter—hell, to exist— led me to write a series of books that would sell hundreds of thousands of copies. I had no idea in the two years it took me to write the book proposal and sell it to a publisher that any of that would happen. I had to authentically follow what was calling. I had to keep getting lost—going back to trying to write screenplays, getting depressed again—and then pick up the trail of comfort that had been whispered to me.

I returned to this story again and again in my mid-forties when I was mired in another *why bother* bog—not because I had been successful, but because *I wanted to remember what it felt like to stop pushing.* I wanted to recall that day I gave up the idea of who I had to be and let what was calling me take me.

I treasure a line from the pre-Socratic philosopher Meno, which Rebecca Solnit quotes in her book *A Field Guide to Getting Lost*: "How will you go about finding that thing the nature of which is totally unknown to you?" To find your next *why bother*, you must not only let go of who you've been, you must also resist creating a new story of who you will become. Both stories are far too small, far too familiar. They contain no mystery, no discovery. Your practice—which again sounds so easy yet is anything but—is to stay open to what will emerge without muting or manipulating what comes to you. The very nature of what you will find is totally unknown to you. In the next chapter, you'll ease in to new experiences and ways of thinking, have conversations that will bring shivers of recognition, experience coincidences that speak to something bigger and more alive than your current identity, and who knows what else? You do this not by insisting that things work out in the way you want; you do this because you consent to being enlivened. Which means no longer hiding behind *it's too late, I'm not good enough or smart enough or young enough.*

It also means not hiding behind success, power, and hard-earned comfort. I've worked with my share of super-successful people trapped by their identities as publisher, fashion designer, activist, surgeon, writer, business powerhouse, neuroscientist. These clients often feel doubly stuck:

there's all they've worked for and accomplished, all the people who depend on them, and there is their own doubt about
what might be more fulfilling. What if they can't do it again?
What if they don't have the talent or the energy or the drive?
What if they are fooling themselves with some "grass is
greener" fantasy?

As you let life re-inspire you, you can't predict what you
will have to give up or learn, or how you will need to change
and stretch. But until you're willing to give up your attachment to who you think you are and what you think you must
do to matter or be a good or successful person, nothing new
can come in. Nothing.

The places where you cling to your identity must be
released, again and again. Imagine who you think you are
as a paper boat holding a candle. The candle is the beauty
and grace of all you have created and stood for and offered
the world. It is night, the breeze soft and fragrant with some
flower you can't name but love the scent of. You lean down
and release your boat into the wide, slow-moving river. All
around you, other people release their boats, boats of all
shapes and sizes. You watch as your tiny craft meanders away
from you. You watch with an ache and a feeling of falling but
you breathe, and you trust that it's going where it needs to
go. Finally, your boat disappears around a bend. You take the
hands of those on either side of you. Together, you turn to
peer into the welcoming darkness.

Reflect

What had you left behind before reading this chapter? It's not about leaving stuff behind 100 percent of the time, but doing it enough that you are considering what would light you up next.

What are you considering leaving behind now? Imagine what freedom might look like, and allow yourself to have it. You have to give yourself permission internally before you can make change on the outside.

How might the natural creative process of living help you distinguish yourself from what you no longer want to bother about? Where can you lean on life to take you forward?

Could there be room for depression, illness, grief, lack of energy, self-doubt, *and* your renewed and reinvented life?

Do you pause when you notice your emotional immune system defending you? Practice pausing.

You're giving yourself the necessary space and freedom needed for true and lasting transformation. Keep your focus there. That's what matters.

———————————

(6)

Ease In

I Matter

Ease in as a stage might feel squishy and frustrating, at least at first. You still aren't taking action on anything in particular. *What's next* isn't clear, or if it is, your energy and resiliency isn't up to it yet and your desire isn't dialed in. That can feel so hard. But I promise, by not getting caught up in the *how*, you're giving yourself the very necessary space and freedom needed for true and lasting transformation. *How* is a boondoggle at this stage.

Anne Truitt wrote in *Daybook: The Journal of an Artist*, "If I wish to be responsible to myself, and I do, I have to pursue my aspirations. In the course of doing so, I find myself confronted by the necessity to recognize my ambition." Ambition has a grasping tone to it, a mood of "I will do anything to get what I want." But consider another definition of ambition: *something you very much want to do*. You very much want to bother again. That is your ambition and for it to happen, you must choose it. Not once, but over and over again. *How* you go about doing that doesn't enter in yet.

Spiritual guide Amy Oscar wrote to me, "I have an answer to why bother. It's this: because I matter. I wouldn't have understood that if I hadn't gone through the dark and difficult struggle of the past ten years. I wouldn't have been able to grasp the deeper teaching under that simple statement: *I matter*. Some people may find comfort in the notion we matter to god or to the angels or to our ancestors or to our children. Me, I find my roots in this: *I matter to myself*."

I matter. Some of us receive this truth from loving caregivers, some of us from a beloved teacher or a book or religion. Others learned at a young age we didn't matter—whether from abuse or discrimination or being told who we were was not good enough. And many of us received the message that we mattered only if we achieved, took care of others, or hid certain parts of our identity and desires. Our mission is to know until the refrain hums sweetly in our minds: *I matter*.

I taught myself I matter through my creative work. Not because I was successful—that taught me the opposite: that I was worthwhile only if I sold books, got speaking gigs, was loved by readers. It wasn't until I discovered *creating* as something I do for myself that I learned I matter.

But creativity is not the only way to experience *you matter*, not at all. Perhaps you know it through being loved as yourself, whether by a person, an animal, or yourself. Perhaps you feel it at the bottom of a deep red rock canyon or by a mountain river where the smell of the wild water returns you to yourself. Perhaps you've touched it during meditation or prayer or dance. Or listening to music. It doesn't matter how or when. It matters that you keep choosing *I matter*.

Perhaps you feel it when you gave up on a creative dream or project like Tracy did when, after spending four years and nearly $100,000 to write a book and build a business, she knew she had to let it all go. Tracy came to understand what she wanted to bother about was her healing and her family. She realized that "what hid behind my inspirational YouTube videos and Insta-perfect snippets was a recovering people pleaser who pushed aside her extreme anxiety, and a lost little girl still grieving the death of her mom. Letting go of my dream seemed like I had given in to not bothering. In fact, it was how I began to understand what was really worth bothering about. What gets me to wake up each day now isn't an Uber waiting to drive me to the set of *Super Soul Sunday*; it's knowing that growth, answers, and a larger contribution lie in my showing up and doing this human gig." It's so damn easy to fall into thinking you matter if you live your dream successfully. I have heard hundreds of stories like Tracy's, where a particular version of the dream became the reason not to bother—and that includes from people who have been tremendously successful. When our story isn't connected to what matters to us, all the money and praise and Instagram followers in the world can't give us a reason to care.

But you might say, "I know *I* matter but what I want to matter *about*, or whom I want to matter *to*, is gone. So I don't care if *I* matter ever again." You can't go back in time—that's a fact. You can never really "get over" loss and tragedy. But if you believe you cannot bother again, then you're saying to yourself that your desires, longings, and hopes are void. You will not allow yourself to care again, to flourish, to discover what's next. Is that fair? You are ceding your present to your past. That's very different from declaring you can't recover or move on. It's not that you are insisting the present be the same as the past. You declare that who are you today is also allowed to flourish. You matter.

Your Anger Matters

"Why do you always have to be so sensitive?"

"You don't know what you're talking about. Stay out of this."

"It doesn't matter to anyone but you."

"You just don't understand how business works. After you've been around awhile, you'll see how it is."

I gathered these statements from friends and readers when I asked if anybody had ever been silenced or shamed for being angry, especially when it came to work or something they cared deeply about.

Starting at a young age, girls are taught that it is not acceptable to own your anger or express it. If we do get angry, we're often labeled ugly, selfish, shrill, hysterical, irrational, overly sensitive, a drama queen, or a high-maintenance bitch. We're dismissed.

We learn to doubt what we see, what we feel, what we value, and what we stand for. We learn to doubt that what we want matters. We learn to ease up on our passion and question our convictions and our experiences. Or as Amy wrote on Facebook, "Now that I think about it, the overall gaslighting [of my anger] was the most toxic. Losing trust in my feelings and experiences after being gaslighted made it so easy to not trust my intuition. That's my road to apathy."

The cost of not being able to express our anger is enormous. Experts from linguists to pain researchers agree we are at higher risk for eating disorders, self-harming, autoimmune disorders, sexual dysfunction, heart disease, certain kinds of cancer, depression, and anxiety. Suppressing our anger does not cause these diseases but can be part of a complex web of factors that contribute to becoming ill.

Being punished for showing anger is one symptom of a far more comprehensive system of oppression we've been fighting for millennia. You live in a world where being a woman often means less—less freedom, less safety, less power, less money—and this knowing shapes your desires and your gumption.

"People who have faith in life are like swimmers who entrust themselves to a rushing river. They neither abandon themselves to its current nor try to resist it. Rather, they adjust their every movement to the watercourse, use it with purpose and skill, and enjoy the adventure."

———————————

BROTHER DAVID STEINDL-RAST,
DEEPER THAN WORDS

I want you to consider this: is it possible your current funk has something to do with being silenced, afraid, or exhausted after pushing against limits for so long or being belittled for doing so? If it was safe to be mad, if you'd been taught to say, "Hell no!" and not expect the world to come crashing down on you, if you believed you had power and opportunities equal to most men, would you be more likely to bother right now or to know what you want to bother about? Is there a disowned fury it might be time to claim as starter fluid for your bothering?

I ask because this is exactly what happened to me.

I was almost sixteen, riding in the back seat of my parents' car, headed home from dinner. Dad was in a good mood because it hadn't rained in two weeks, good for his construction company. Before I go any further in this story, I should tell you I adored my dad and put him on a pedestal. He was a loving, kind man who lived by a high standard of ethics and took excellent care of his family and many employees. He was also a chauvinist and a racist.

Maybe it was Dad's good mood or the orange-pearl sunset or the two glasses of chardonnay Mom drank with dinner, but something made her speak up that night in a way that changed the course of my life.

"Doyle," she said, "one of the girls I play tennis with, she works part time at a gift store out at Cedar Pointe Plaza." Her voice sounded off—small, tentative, unlike her. It made me pay attention. "You know the one, next to Pawnbroker Grill?

They're looking for someone to help in the store and maybe, later, with interior design."

I immediately got what she was saying. My mom wanted to do something outside of making us gourmet dinners, playing tennis, and being a candy striper at Martin Memorial Hospital, and I wanted that for her too. She was smart and beautiful, and I'd always wanted her to help me sell the most Girl Scout Cookies and throw epic parties.

I leaned forward. "Mom, that's so groovy. That'll be so fun for you." I looped my arms around her headrest and hugged her.

She patted my hand and I sat back. "I would only work part time when Jenny's in school," she said, looking at Dad while she played with her pearls. "It's very flexible."

I pictured Mom in the shop. It was in the ritzier part of town, near the ocean. I could see her wearing something chic, her frosted hair fluffed high, arranging seashell candy dishes and crinkly cellophane bags of cranberry-and-dried-orange-slice potpourri. In my mind, she was already running the store, decorating oceanfront homes, pirouetting on one heel, hand to her pretty mouth. She'd be in demand. Everybody would want Betty to consult with them. I thrilled to my vision.

Dad sped up through the yellow light. "Absolutely not," he said. His tone made my stomach clench. "I forbid it." He took the left onto A1A too fast. I rolled against the door. "I want you available when I want you," he added. "If I want to pick up and travel, go out to dinner, I want you there. I don't work hard all day long to come home and have you gone." He shook his head. "I forbid it."

Did I lean forward and scream at Dad? Take Mom's side against him? I so want to remember I did. I think I did, but I'm not sure. All I know for sure is even now, forty years after the fact, twelve years since my dad died, my anger at how he stopped my mom is almost as bright and hot as it was that night.

I vibrated with outrage. Before the car even came to a full stop, I jumped out, slammed the door, bolted to my room, called my best friend Barb, my fingers missing keys on the keypad I was shaking so much. I switched into my well-mannered voice when her mom answered. "Hello Mrs. Glascock, this is Jennifer, how are you tonight?" then flipped back to rage when Barb picked up the extension. "I'm running away and you have to help me. You need to take me to the bus station in the morning. I'll go to Grandma in Indiana." I told her I can't live in the same house with a father who imprisoned my mother.

But I did not run away. Dad said something mollifying the next morning at breakfast. Mom said she didn't want to be tied down to a job after all. There was probably a party that weekend I didn't want to miss. I bristled and postured in front of my friends about how angry I was, but slowly I forgot about it.

But while writing this book, the memory came roaring out and onto the page. It was suddenly clear: this incident had sparked my entire reason to center my career on empowering women! I had wanted to help my mom but I couldn't, so I helped other women. The feeling I get when I hear about people not bothering, not creating what they want? It is the same feeling I had in the back of my parents' car, a shocking tightness in my chest and throat, a low roaring in my ears. If I put words to it, they would be "Get out of our way. Don't you dare try to stop us." But because we are often blind to what shapes us, I had no idea why I was doing my work. I never knew the source of my desire.

Over the years, I diluted my message and voice and often dismissed my work. Even when people told me I had changed their lives, inwardly I scoffed. In some ways, I did to myself what my dad did to my mom: I shut myself down. But when I wrote that story about mom, I began to re-experience my anger and the raw connection to my work, and that infused me with an entirely new feeling of purpose. I now know why I do what I do, and I have committed to doing it more honestly and unreservedly.

Your anger can tell you the truth about why you bother and what you want to bother about. It can reveal what has to change so you have the freedom and dignity to flourish. Anger can lead you to understand what you care about and how you haven't allowed yourself to own that caring. Your anger can furnish you the energy to work so there is room for you in the world. It can help you roar, "Get out of my way."

I'm not suggesting you stay angry all the time. That would be hell on your body and spirit. But to return to life, you must stop silencing and policing yourself. Research shows that African American girls maintain higher self-esteem than boys through high school, the only group of girls to do so. One theory is that Black mothers are less likely to teach their daughters to silence themselves, swallow their anger, and play nice because the cost to their safety is too high in a racist world. You can't collude with a system that wants to hold you back, hurt you, diminish you, and dismiss you. You can't collude if you want to bother again.

There is a clear connection between your spark being lit again and the culture's beliefs and norms silencing you. Suppressing your anger teaches you to be a pessimist, resigned to powerlessness, turning your rage on yourself instead of on the systems that need to change. Claiming your anger and channeling it in healthy ways can feel destabilizing and forbidden at first, but with practice, access to what pisses you off can bring the motivation and energy you need.

I Can Have Grit without the Grind

The phrase "self-compassionate grit" popped into my head in the middle of a yoga class during my darkest *why bother* stretch. I was struggling with my mysterious back ailment that sidelined me from physical activity for months at a time. When I could move, I had to be extra mindful of my tendency to do too much and then reinjure myself. I was carefully stretching back into reverse warrior when I heard an inner voice quip, "Grit without self-compassion is just grind."

I thought, "God, don't I know it!" I was excellent at grind, especially when I was miserable and lost. Do *something* even if it wasn't what I wanted—that was my default. I was like a wind-up toy that wouldn't stop trying to go somewhere even though I was in the corner, my little plastic head bouncing off the wall.

Self-compassionate grit felt very different in my body. To treat myself with the same care I did my daughter, my girl-friends, my students *while* I stayed engaged and in action. This *while* was a giant revelation for me. When I was floundering, I confused *grit* with *grind*, with relentless, pointless busyness or endless hustling to prove my worth. I told myself at least I was doing something and that's what mattered. But when you don't know why you're doing what you're doing, then grinding away is terribly demoralizing. In fact, grind by itself can send you into *why bother* even though you may love your life. Grind can trap you in a box of lifeless possibil-ities, in a wearying pattern of trying to get it right, trying to please everybody and keep up with the pace of your job or the demands you've let creep in. Do this long enough and *why bother* will poison what once brought you satisfaction, beauty, and meaning.

Self-compassionate grit steadies you. It helps you hold space for what will enter next. It gives you earplugs of love when the self-protective whispers of your emotional immune system try to convince you to go back, give up, stop this process. For some of us, *why bother* gets louder when we reengage with life. A voice hectors, "What the hell do you think will be different this time? This is madness. Get back to what you know." Better to stay busy or checked out than to open yourself to new life. Self-compassionate grit is like a great boss or friend who listens carefully while you whine and then gently and firmly challenges you to do it anyway.

It can be easy to confuse self-compassion with shadow comforts; I know I have. *Shadow comforts* is a term I coined when writing my first book in the early '90s. It's anything you do in the name of self-care or, in my case, self-compassion. But instead of helping you stay engaged with life, or relaxing and recharging you so you become stronger, shadow comforts leave you feeling worse about yourself. It isn't necessarily what you do, but why you do it and how it makes you feel.

I'd preached about shadow comforts for nearly thirty years. I thought I knew intimately how these substitutes showed up for me. But I hadn't noticed I'd decided being self-compassionate equaled numbing out, say with murder mysteries and cookies, even if those cookies were organic and made with coconut sugar. Sometimes mysteries and cookies recharged me, but more often my self-nurturing choices left me feeling like crap, spiraling downward.

Self-compassionate grit offers an alternative to numbing out or grinding yourself into a pile of rubble. You acknowledge that engaging in life again is difficult and scary, that you don't have the energy, you don't know what's next, *and* you stay alert and willing to engage. You hold both.

Remembering that you aren't alone or somehow uniquely flawed because you feel blah or unsure life is worth living— that's self-compassion. Realizing what's at stake is your connection and devotion to life itself and it's up to you to connect with life again—that's grit. Self-compassionate grit is determination *with* self-kindness. It's saying to yourself, "Get off the couch, honey, right now" *while* staying on your own side. It's small steps taken with steady faith. Self-compassionate grit fosters the spiritual dignity you need to open to your rediscovery. It helps you stay alert and relaxed, ready to collaborate with the natural process of life.

As this process unfolds, we'll go into more detail about how self-compassionate grit can help you bother. But first, it's time for wonder.

I Wonder

Wonder defies a neat explanation. There is no step-by-step process to capture it, but here are a few aspects I have recognized. Wonder...

- is the inspiration behind bothering again
- refuses to know
- declines to figure anything out

- does not analyze, fix, or prescribe
- sees beyond all frozen feelings of inevitability
- communicates in flashes, images, shivers, "live wire" dreams, slivers of ideas, a line from a song you can't get out of your head
- flirts with grace and sleeps with mystery
- is never less than present
- has no finish or end
- does not recognize difficulty as a problem but a summons
- doesn't care who you think you are
- inveigles you to remember life is by its very nature creative
- sweeps fatalism, cynicism, pessimism, parochialism, and all other -isms up in a whirlwind
- disturbs you; pokes you awake at three in the morning; causes you to try things, say things, think things that make your friends or your kids say, "Who are you?"
- communicates in questions
- knows what you love can always be born again in a new form
- doesn't care where it takes you, only that it does

Wonder awakens. It offers freshness. It lives beyond the known and puts you in your new story. Yet if you had told me, deep in the murk of my soul's apathy, to wonder, I would have told you to fuck off. Wonder can seem weak medicine against the convincing know-it-all certainty of *why bother*. That's why I introduced you to self-compassionate grit first. You must hold your mind and heart steadily open as you wonder. You must be alert to the alligator snap of "How stupid" and "Who cares?" when a desire stirs in you. Your brain is trying to save you from wonder, which it regards as uncertainty, because it equates wonder with danger and death.

Meg, a member of my online community, the weekly Oasis, was struggling with *why bother* on several fronts— writing, dating... and striving toward wanting anything again because she felt like nothing ever paid off. I gave her some suggestions for getting unstuck and here's what she told me a year and half later: "You said that when things are uncertain, our brains want certainty, and 'nothing is ever going to get better' at least *sounds* like certainty, even if it's total conjecture and there's no grounds for it... That negative certainty is what our brains offer us when we're grasping for solid ground."

You must drop your expectations, the kind of expectation that everything will work out the way you want it. That's falling back into what you know and who you think you must be. Wonder brings a different kind of expectation: that goodness, caring, and liveliness are yours to have and enjoy.

Every time I've gotten lost, I started back toward life with wonder leading the way. That's where I began again. Wonder moved this small-town Southern girl across the country to L.A. to attend film school at USC, knowing no one and having made only a handful of short films. "I wonder what it would be like to lead a creative life." Wonder came calling when I stopped insisting screenwriting was my only path in life. "I wonder what 'women's comfort' means?" Wonder prodded me when I became unexpectedly pregnant and moved out of L.A. to Santa Barbara. "What would it be like to find a place I love to live and to belong to a place?" Wonder took me to a mentor's house in Crested Butte when I was again blank and stuck, and I wondered if she could help me like she had years before on a women's canoe trip that felt mythical. Wonder came when I heeded the call to write fiction and coach creative women. With my forays into making art. In my romantic adventures after my divorce. In moving to Colorado. In wondering about the dead-end moments in life that eventually led to this book.

Wonder did not, however, deliver me to where I wanted to be. That's not wonder's role. Wonder eased me back into life. From there, I had to learn other skills to propel me forward. Sometimes I progressed and sometimes I didn't but that doesn't negate the importance of wonder. Without honoring those inklings fostered by "I wonder..." nothing would have changed.

Think about your life: is there an absence of wonder?

What do you keep spurning? Turning your back on? Not even letting get a toehold in your attention? Make Grandma's cookie recipe. Find your cousin and ask what she remembers about that summer. Write about your sister's illness. Drive across the country by yourself. Learn to ride a unicycle. Study Sufism. Learn a poem a week by heart.

The point is to pay attention, then follow. It's stopping the automatic, often barely conscious repudiation.

"I don't eat sugar, why make her cookie recipe?"

"I haven't talked to Nila Jo since we were twelve and I wouldn't even know what to ask her."

"It'll be too painful to write about Sue being sick; I can't go there."

Pay attention to what you are shrugging off. When you shrug, you collude with *why bother*.

When my friend Molly was feeling detached and bored about her work and her place in the community, she didn't force herself to do anything or "fix" the issue. She kept doing what she normally did: coaching clients, loving her husband, planting her garden. And she kept checking in: what appealed? What seemed like fun? She opened up to "I wonder" in different ways every day. Her wonder led to her desire. She assumed nothing about how she was feeling was permanent or meant anything about her future or her value as a human.

I, on the other hand, worried for her. I was sure she was checking out too much, not earning enough money, not marketing her business sufficiently. Thankfully, she never asked me what I thought.

She volunteered at a local theater company doing lighting design, something she hadn't done since college, and it required her to be out past her bedtime and to deal with

"Wonder is
the heaviest
element on the
periodic table.
Even a tiny fleck
of it stops time."

DIANE ACKERMAN,

THE RAREST OF THE RARE

creative conflicts and personalities. Instead of that making it a deal-breaker for her, as it might have in the past, Molly stayed open. She became intensely interested in racial injustice. She volunteered for an organization that supported at-risk kids. She became a hospice volunteer. She dove deep into a new spiritual path.

Molly didn't push the river, nor did she ignore its current. She paid attention to what seemed interesting even if she wasn't sure she would like it or where it would lead. She dropped her habit of critiquing and passing judgment—not entirely, but enough to wonder.

You already know how to wonder. You have known since birth. You know how to marvel, to part the curtain of everyday life, of the same old, of assumptions. Why waste any more energy telling yourself you don't have time or asking what's the point? Marry self-compassionate grit with wonder to get your *why bother* back.

Wonder will not give you directions. Wonder doesn't tell you what is yours to care about next. *Wonder's job is to breathe you to life.* Wonder comes and it goes, and each time, it leaves you more awake.

When you are lost in *why bother*, you might be telling yourself bothering is too costly, too much trouble, or pointless because things will end up right back where they started. Wonder flies right past these tired old defenses. It expands your emotional immune system so you have more awareness and less reactivity.

Hurrying along checking things off your to-do list makes it harder for wonder to exhilarate you back toward caring. Give wonder enough time to seduce you.

Wonder may come to you more easily in a new environment, so by all means take the trip to Patagonia or the Isle of Skye. But know that wonder is also waiting for you in your kitchen, in the books you've already read, on your best friend's face, on your daily walk. For fifteen years, I walked three or four times a week along a dirt road through a forest near my home. One summer afternoon, I decided to see what I hadn't seen before. Part of me thought, "This is stupid. Maybe I'll spot a patch of new mushrooms or something like that, but this is a boring walk and you have a boring life." Five minutes later, I spotted a water tower. A two-story water tower set back from the road about fifteen yards. I had never seen this water tower. I stopped. I stared. "Is that new?" But the tower was furred with moss and a touch of graffiti. It had been there all these years, and I had never noticed.

The startle of a water tower, what did it do for me? It startled me out of the certainty that I knew. It made me wonder what else I was missing because of all my *knowing*. It made me hunger for more freshness, for more life. The only thing that stands between you and the freshness of wonder is allowing yourself this grace, giving yourself over to the beauty.

Trusting Yourself Enough to Wonder

If you're second-guessing what you're wondering about and why it matters, if there is something better to wonder about, or if you will dither around forever, this is exactly when self-trust comes into play. Self-trust is the act of paying attention to what you're feeling, sensing, and noticing rather than reflexively looking outside yourself for guidance or trying to "get it right," whatever that means. Self-trust is the habit of asking yourself, "What do I know?" and "What do I want?" and giving yourself time to feel your way into your next small step. It's having faith in your own experiences.

Self-trust is not arrogance or a mystical faith in your intuition or a puffed-up "That's just the way I am." It's about touching what Buddhism calls your basic goodness; in Christian lineages, divine likeness; in Hinduism, Atman; and I'm sure other traditions have their own equivalents. It's experiencing how you are naturally kind and loving, how you possess an innate warmth, tenderness, and empathy. Actively noticing your fundamental goodness makes it easier to trust yourself.

Experiencing your basic goodness is also an act of empowerment, as Anne pointed out to me during a retreat. She had been taught, as many of us have been, that she wanted too much, asked for too much, spoke up too much. But when she was in touch with her intrinsic kindness, she realized something important: "When I trust I am basically good, it means I can speak from that place, instead of having to prove myself or defend myself. There's nothing to prove or defend!" Knowing your basic goodness makes it less fraught to share your concerns or voice your outrage, which builds your self-trust.

Speaking from our experience is a profound act of self-trust, and it's something I'm working on. I hold an ancient imprint of shame around being stupid. This can instantly turn into either prickly self-defense or a stony silence in any situation, say when my husband, Bob, and I disagree because I'm not sure I know enough to speak up. When I can trust myself in these moments to say what I feel while also trusting my basic goodness, everything softens. When I remember my innate goodness, I move out of shame and from there I can trust my own experience enough to recognize and verbalize it.

Self-trust keeps you out of the victim story because you are not giving your power away to others through blame or by hoping "they" will tell you what to do or how to feel. Self-trust reminds you that bothering again is worthwhile because it brings *you* back into life, not because it fixes something about you that's broken or makes the world a better place. Self-trust declares, "I value my thoughts and opinions because I am alive."

Wonder flourishes with self-trust because wonder needs you to pay attention. You can't wonder if you are asking someone else, "Is this wonder worthy?" You take yourself out of the moment and away from yourself. You can't feel awe if you're worried you might look silly. You can't be curious if you are second-guessing your every desire.

What you bother about must arise honestly from within you. *You can only care about what is yours to care about.* You can't fake it. You can't force it. You can't borrow your direction from someone else, not from a partner or a church, not from your parents or your job. Nor can you hold on to what no longer brings you alive, even if you once cherished it and you mourn its passing. Wonder wakes you up and connects you with what is authentically awe-inspiring or at least slightly interesting to you right *now*. It brings you face-to-face with life and helps you remember, even if only for a few breaths, "Oh yes, I am here, and I can trust myself to pay attention to what I care about." But without self-trust, wonder withers.

Still, you may protest, "But I already found out who I was, why do I need to do it again?" You might stamp your foot and refuse. But when you look at the wide world of stories, you might reconsider. How many movies and TV shows and books have you watched or read about people getting lost, waylaid, defeated, and having to find their way again? Why are you any different from all the other humans? You too are in a state of perennial formation. Allowing that formation, wondering about it, trusting it, is what this quest is all about.

You may feel you never chose a *why bother* that was entirely yours or that fit you. Maybe you've been trying to borrow what you can't borrow. You may have a sinking feeling you can never find a path that is truly yours. I wish I could lend you my faith because from where I sit, having worked with thousands of people, I know that's categorically false. I know every single person has so many things that are theirs to care about, to bring into being, to enjoy, to share. But you don't have to know what I know. You only need to trust what brings you alive, what makes you wonder, now.

I love Elana's story of how she started to wonder, to try things, and to build her self-trust—it's not about lightning bolts or surety, it's about being willing. "Last year, after my last work contract ended, one that I had held great hope for, the weight of disappointment and disillusionment threatened to flatten me. I was filled with anxiety, self-doubt, self-criticism, insecurity. I had to move myself and my son in with my family, I gained weight, and all I wanted to do was lie facedown on my bed and scream.

> Get more pointers on self-trust including a self-trust guided meditation at jenniferloudon.com/whybother.

"What makes me bother when all I want to do some days is run away and become a Buddhist nun is the faint hope that I can create something new and authentically me—if I just start. The merest possibility that I can feel empowerment, joy, and belief in my innate gifts again—if I just start. The ember inside of me that I turn toward when I bother, if I catch this ember and cradle and feed it, I can show myself and my son that, no matter what, honoring our creativity and our desire is worth it for its own sake. So I start."

So you have started. And whatever hurt and heartbreak and bad advice, whatever glory and beauty and love got you here, self-trust will keep you awake as you are becoming.

Playing with Your Habits

Have you ever said about someone, "She is such a creature of habit"? What does that mean? Perhaps that the force of habit is eclipsing anything spontaneous or new from having a chance.

Habits and routines can be immensely helpful. They help you manage the otherwise overwhelming amount of stuff you must deal with every day, all the decisions, activities, and relationships you juggle. They can help you turn your life around, offer you stability and clarity when you are trying to do something hard like give up smoking or make time for your creative work. My habit of writing first thing in the morning with latte in hand, for instance, has been hard won and I don't want to give it up.

But habits and routines can also stifle, become about choosing comfort over wonder, what's familiar over what discombobulates, reacting over listening, productivity over being.

Case in point: I wrote part of this book during a five-day solo retreat in a tiny cabin at 10,600 feet in the Rockies. No internet, sketchy cell service, and the only person I saw for the five days was the snowplow guy. I came to immerse myself in this book, to escape distraction, and to follow my creative rhythm.

But what I did instead—without at first realizing it, which is the power and danger of routine—was immediately create a morning schedule. Let my dog outside, make a fire, put the kettle on for coffee, feed dog, sit on the couch and drink coffee until my neurons fired enough for me to write. And about a day into the retreat, I declared an audacious goal: to write 16,000 words (crappy first draft words) and run sixteen miles over the course of my retreat. My morning routine and my writing/running goals quickly hijacked my intention to immerse myself in creative flow. There I was in my remote mountain cabin feeling driven and stiff, my teeth clenched. I came on retreat to slow down and embody the message of this book, and I was doing everything but.

I could physically sense how my rigidity was cutting off the regenerative power of my rare time alone, in my tight jaw and my jackdaw-like inner chatter. The current of the book, the spirit of love behind it, wanted to come through me but I was afraid. Controlling life's energy with rigid routines was one of the familiar ways my emotional immune system worked to defend me. I've always done this when I get close to what I want: go into hyperdrive.

But this time, once I realized what I was doing, I turned to self-compassionate grit. I put my hand on my heart and told myself, "This retreat and wanting this book to work are hard for you. This is scary." I made my exhales longer than my inhales to calm my nervous system. I reminded myself, "Everybody has different ways they make themselves stay safe. This is yours. And you can make another choice because you are safe. You are enough." I went outside to stare at the three mountains that ringed the cabin, blue in the snowy, late afternoon light. The silence beat against my eardrums. I searched the snow for the fox that had visited me the evening before, but even her footprints had vanished, covered by that morning's snowfall. I relaxed into the awe of the view. I put on a song and danced on the deck, letting my body remind me how to be present, how to open to life. My mind couldn't do that for me, but my body could.

For the rest of the retreat, I paused when my ambition and goals pulled at me. I paid close attention to how my emotional immune system was working overtime. I allowed myself to ache with how much I cared about making this book the best it can be, for you and for me. I placed my attention there, again and again, instead of on my fear that I couldn't make it work. I asked, "I wonder what the book wants...?" Over and over, I experimented with dropping my habitual response to blocking life.

Reflect

Imagine that all the thoughts and feelings of not bothering are in your right hand. Take a breath and let those become real to your body. Imagine all the stirrings and flutterings of interest, enthusiasm, wonder, and caring are gathered in your left hand. Feel those for twice as long as you did the feelings of not bothering, apathy, lostness, and

blahness. Easing in is not about denying *why bother*
feelings or thoughts that continue to show up or trying
to power through them; it's about simultaneously placing
your attention on where the opposite is present and alive.

Are you allowing wonder to open your eyes, perhaps in
the most ordinary and mundane of situations?

How is anger showing you what you care about? How
does it remind you that you matter?

How could wonder and anger inspire you to trust yourself?

What's one stifling but comforting habit you could
give up?

If self-compassionate grit could talk, what would she say
to you about getting your bother on?

The grounding grace of inner stillness is always inside you, waiting to receive you.

———————————

(7)

Settle

The Art of Settling Down

What if the only hurdle in your way to being immersed in life—knowing what you want to bother about—is stopping? Resting. Rooting down into being.

If there is one reason people don't find their way to being fulfilled, to living the deeper life they crave, it is because they refuse to settle. You know how to; you just don't remember that you do.

Settling is a complete stop of hectic, grasping, breathless, desperate *doing*. It's stepping out of the digital hurly-burly, the family drama, the inner drama; stepping away from figuring things out, from self-improvement, from ambition—heck, even from learning new things. For example, every time a former colleague of mine got close to figuring out what she really wanted, she signed up for another course or certification, instead of dwelling in and trusting what she already knew.

Settling can happen on vacation, by catching up on your sleep, by meditating, or by taking a retreat. Note that you can emerge from any of these just as frazzled and far away from yourself as before. Settling takes intention and focus but not effort. It is not to be confused with settling for *less*, which is what we do when we don't know why we bother.

You might call settling stillness, getting quiet, being present, or taking a Sabbath. Those are all good terms and I choose "settling" because it reminds me to come back into my body and spiritual gravity, and let go of doing. Settling down signals that I decline to jack myself up. It reminds me that settling is an action I take, a choice.

When you settle, you come into immediate contact with one of the most potent forces for change: the grounding grace of inner stillness. It's always inside you, waiting to receive you. You've experienced it many times, perhaps floating in a warm pool, before a big presentation, reading poetry, after having sex, climbing a hard pitch, hiking, sitting on the beach watching the waves, listening to a friend or client in crisis. Pamela told me she settles before every surgery she performs: "I never considered I could do the same at other times, for myself and not just in service to my patients."

I've got to come clean before I write another word about settling down: every one of my *why bother* times turned toxic and stuck around far longer than necessary because I couldn't get still and wait. I had to get back to doing, to being somebody. By leaping ahead, I truncated the natural process. I was the kid who couldn't wait for the cookies to cool and always burned her mouth.

I knew in my twenties, during my first lost time, what I needed to do. I heard that small voice repeat, "Take a break." Yes, I listened to the call to stop—for a hot second—and then I went straight back to scrambling, writing a new screenplay with a friend that was so bad, my agent wouldn't even try to sell it. I let a grasping frantic energy own me. I wish I could have put a cool cloth on my forehead and said, "Settle down. Inspiration is in the stillness."

"Sure, no problem, waiting, being a chrysalis and all, love it, super spiritual, I'm so cool with this . . . Wait, a day has passed and nothing is happening . . . Shouldn't something be happening? This is so boring . . ."

And then *screw it*. Off I would go. I would do this day after day, settling down a little bit and then distracting myself—with men, with drinking, with fantasies about being a famous writer, and later with technology, clients, and students. Finally, I would get sick of it and make an often-snap decision about what was next, uninformed by my true desire. Which only set me up to do the whole thing again in a few years' time.

I did this in the aftermath of being on *The Oprah Winfrey Show*, moving from Santa Barbara to the Pacific Northwest, divorcing Chris, and smaller moments as well. Each time I tried to settle, but I couldn't. In every major *why bother* moment of my life, I started out wondering, knowing full well I needed to settle down, and then I freaked out and

"Our culture invariably supposes that action and accomplishment are better than rest, that something—anything—is better than doing nothing … Because we do not rest, we lose our way. We miss the compass points that would show us where to go, we bypass the nourishment that would give us succor … For want of rest, our lives are in danger."

———————————

WAYNE MULLER, SABBATH

rushed back into doing whatever felt good enough or likely to get me what I thought I wanted.

It's a tricky stage, this one. The first stages—*leave behind, ease in*—give you at least a little something to do. This stage is all about *not* doing. To ignore, for months, years, or even decades, the yearning to get quiet allows the demands of life and other people to overtake or cancel out your own desires. Or you become so depleted that *why bother* sometimes comes calling not because you aren't doing what you care about, but because you're doing more than you can sustain. Settling allows you to catch up with yourself and to fill yourself up in the way that only deep inner stillness can. To take inventory of what matters to you *and* what is sustainable. To immerse yourself in the depths of what brings you alive simply because you are alive, not because doing so serves a purpose or helps someone else.

What happens for too many of us is what I did. You get close to giving yourself the time and space you crave, you start to let go of what is too much or not fulfilling, and then either distract yourself with chores or work or *Candy Crush Saga* or someone calls and you think, "How much energy will this take? I can do this one little meeting, surely." Or you go backward and do more of what you know. Or you convince yourself too many people depend on you to even consider changing course. Or that your parents will be so disappointed if you declare you want something different than the path they've laid out for you.

To go through your metamorphosis, to discern what to bother and not bother about, and to find the energy to do so, you must stop running and doing and scheming and earning your keep by pleasing and giving and managing and over-providing. You must realize there is an expenditure of life energy in every activity and you only have so much to give.

Why do we starve ourselves of what we so badly want and so dearly know we need if we are to care and thrive again? Because settling down requires us to be with ourselves and to face the fear that we won't like what we find. To outsmart our brains that want to defend us and are so easily snared by technology. To rebel against the culture that has named productivity our god.

I've treasured this quotation from *The Heroine's Journey* by Maureen Murdock for thirty years: "When a woman stops doing, she must learn how to simply be. Being is not a luxury; it is a discipline. The heroine must listen carefully to her true inner voice. That means silencing the other voices anxious to tell her what to do. She must be willing to hold the tension until the new form emerges. Anything less aborts growth, denies change, and reverses transformation. Being takes courage and demands sacrifice."

For a list of books about people settling down and listening, like *Gift from the Sea* by Anne Morrow Lindbergh, May Sarton's diaries, *Plain and Simple* by Sue Bender, and *Deep Water Passage* by Ann Linnea, visit jenniferlouden.com/whybother.

Does that sound daunting, even grim? Why would you go to all that trouble? *Because you have no choice.* You can fool yourself that you do, you can try to half-ass this phase, or put it off like I tried, but it won't go away. And if my experience is any sign, life will return with more vehemence, demanding to know what you will bother about and what you won't. Why waste the time and energy?

Without settling down, the lassitude of *why bother* can take over your life even if nothing is missing and even if nothing needs to change. Your life may in fact be thoroughly satisfying but you've been absent from it for so long that you no longer understand what satisfaction is—and you won't, not until you settle down.

If you continue to stay busy and hectic with over-providing and helicopter parenting and keeping your body and house perfect, with checking the news and texting and refining your personal brand on Instagram, you won't have the energy or deep attention to know desire and to create your new story. You won't be able to form a complex, nuanced thought; to follow the soft stirrings of wonder; to act on what nudges you to delve deeper. Your sense of reality, of self, of depth will keep slipping through your fingers. You'll keep dodging the questions of what's up, what's off, what do I want? You'll keep busy, stay numb, be productive—because it's easier. But all the while the questions will grow heavier in your gut. You'll keep staving off your discontent until it takes over your life.

How can you learn that *being* is a discipline and not a luxury? Perhaps by questioning the various injunctions to always be productive: "I should text my daughter, check on Mom, practice Spanish, protest the government, start the soup for dinner, do some sit-ups." Maybe being looks like quietly watching the birds at your bird feeder or journaling about your stirrings of wonder or taking a long stroll, not a power walk. Maybe it looks like sitting quietly sipping your tea, instead of rushing to put away the clean dishes, walk the dog, listen to the news.

We sprint away from our grief, our sadness, our insecurities, our heartbreaks, our disappointments, our fear of being seen; in doing so, we hold at bay what we most want. We doom ourselves to the flat side of *why bother*. We tell ourselves it's too hard, there is no time, it's too painful, or we don't know how. All the while, life tries to get through to us, to love us awake. When you're squirming away from what's here now—which most of us do a million times a day—it's impossible to hear what wants to emerge.

It's normal to worry that *being* is a fancy word for torpor, for sinking into the couch, for falling back into resignation. But when I kindly welcome my experience, question my addiction to productivity, and trust my desires, I can't also be a hopeless, self-doubting computer potato. As long as I keep engaging with *any* part of the creative process, life rushes right in to inspire me.

Settling spirals through your refashioning in long strands and short pauses. You rest, you wonder, you try to go back

"Why is everything rushed? When did quick become the standard of our desires? Why is fast-paced given authority over a slow, steady flow? It's time to detox from grind culture. It's time to rest."

THE NAP MINISTRY

to your old life, you stop and settle down, you welcome, you follow desire, you freak out—and on it goes until you look back and realize, "I'm through. I'm reshaped. I know how to bother again."

Be Truly Absorbed

If you've tried settling down and found it impossible to stay with this stage, don't give up. Your nervous system is likely hijacked by near constant activation, a bombardment of stimuli that you're not built to handle. And if there is one single thing that stands between most people and finding their desire to bother again, it's their pinging here and zinging everywhere, scattered, jangled, and interrupted at every turn.

If you're living like most humans in the industrialized world, you *must* address how technology, complexity, information glut, and the sheer number of things you do each day are blocking your ability to bother again. Dampening it and attenuating it. Like Dug the dog in one of my favorite movies, *Up*, you focus on wonder, on settling down, on what's calling you and then *Ball! Squirrel!* off you go.

Here's the chilling truth: you can dribble away the rest of your life in a distracted, fragmented rush and never attend to what you most want to bother about. Or as the writer and neurologist Oliver Sacks wrote in a *New Yorker* essay, "Every minute, every second, has to be spent with one's device clutched in one's hand. Those trapped in this virtual world are never alone, never able to concentrate and appreciate in their own way, silently. They have given up, to a great extent, the amenities and achievements of civilization: solitude and leisure, the sanction to be oneself, truly absorbed, whether in contemplating a work of art, a scientific theory, a sunset, or the face of one's beloved." To be truly absorbed is to bother.

Yet while writing this chapter, I must have checked email two dozen times. I missed a scheduled call with my online community, which meant I needed to reschedule my guest and make sure my community knew what happened. I emailed my guest first thing in the morning but then, instead of being absorbed in writing this—writing what I deeply care about—I kept hitting refresh on my email to see if she'd responded. Even as my mind said, "This is insane," my brain did what brains do: scan for threats and for diversion. Your brain knows how to focus but not so much that you don't see the dangerous thing coming, or that you don't miss out on something advantageous. That wasn't a big deal for most of our history, but nowadays? Yikes.

I alternate between being frightened by this behavior and pissed off at myself and the engineers who designed all the addictive technologies that surround me. I know the life I want is not staring at a screen or hurtling between items on my to-do list. I also know the human brain is not built to ignore, at least not for long, email, news feeds, or the little pop-up on Netflix that says, "Next episode starting in 5, 4, 3, 2..." That's because we seek the anticipation of pleasurable rewards. We're curious animals who want to know what's around the corner. That's why we look up, hours later, bleary-eyed, having gone down the internet rabbit hole, scrolled through shopping sites, or binge-watched *The Great British Baking Show*. It's why I kept checking email to see if my guest had responded.

If I do this now and then, no big deal. But when I was in my *why bother* times, months were eaten up by this pointless clicking. It made it impossible to break the trance of resignation and regret, to find what was missing. It made it impossible to *settle*.

It's not only the lure of technology that keeps you from the discipline of being. It's also how much is demanded of you each day. It's not your imagination—you *are* being forced or at least pressured to do more than ever. For many professions, the rise of email and services like Slack has blurred the line between being at work and being off work. The growing wealth gap has translated into less economic mobility, meaning it's harder to make the money you need to keep pace with the rising cost of living. Raising kids has become a competitive sport. Heck, reading the ingredients in my face cream and comparing it to the list of ingredients that cause cancer takes time and effort.

Our brains like all this juggling, all this doing. It's reassuring. Even if the bigger question of *why bother* eludes or terrifies you, hey, you still remembered to buy dog food, write the report, and make gluten-free, nut-free cookies for the school party. So there's that.

Despite that; it is entirely possible to work with your brain and find stillness and perspective. You need not become a Luddite or move off the grid. And you will *not* wait for life to get simpler, your job to get better, your student debt to be paid off, your kids to get older (unless they are babies, in which case give yourself a break—your *why bother* mood may be sleep deprivation), or your parents to move out of the family house and into assisted living. *There is no golden age of spaciousness and stillness.* Waiting for one means you're mortgaging this life for a future that may never arrive.

Most people mightily resist this settling stage. They think, "I don't need it, let's get to the business at hand," or "I did it for ten minutes, that's enough." Settling in with yourself doesn't fit into a slot on your to-do list. But without a calm(er) nervous system, you'll be right back on your phone or folding clothes or answering an email or calling a client. You *must* give your body time to come out of rushing and doing to remember you are not prey. Because that's what the older parts of your brain believe. Prey doesn't relax very much. Have you ever watched a herd of deer, and how often they scan their environment for predators? Not conducive to finding your desire or your next creative expression. What settling does is give you a way to get past how you are built—and habituated—to respond and, combined with easing in, immerse you in the experience of being more in tune and alive.

If you are in real danger—whether from an abusive spouse, looming eviction, unemployment, custody issues with kids, a frightening health diagnosis—you can't relax, and pressuring yourself to do so is cruel. Your *why bother* right now is taking action to secure your safety. You will locate desire once your physical body and well-being, or those of the people you directly take care of, are no longer in danger.

As the American Buddhist nun Pema Chödrön noted in *When Things Fall Apart*, "Things are always in transition, if we could only realize it. Nothing ever sums itself up in the way that we like to dream about. The off-center, in-between state is an ideal situation, a situation in which we don't get caught and we can open our hearts and minds beyond limit. It's a very tender, nonaggressive, open-ended state of affairs." What is "safety" for you, given your current situation? If you know you can stay in your home, for example, for another month and you've done your home hunting for the day, then would settling down be safe to do? If you are safe in a friend's house in another state, is it okay to spend some time getting quiet? Staying in a state of hyperarousal will not serve you or your health, so it's very important to keep asking when it's okay to settle down.

Having a difficult time settling is not your fault. It's a symptom of the technological and societal changes that our brains and bodies are not adapted for, but who are we kidding? Settling down has never been easy. We're social creatures, we've always had lives to tend to, and being quiet with ourselves has always taken effort. Nevertheless, who is going to determine your future—Netflix, your boss, your pet? Settling down is an act of soul resistance, and your life depends on it.

I Have to Move

Settling is not about being still in your body. You might settle by riding your bike in nature, practicing yoga, or hiking. In my last *why bother* period, I needed regular movement practices for my well-being, but I had to be intentional about what I did. For example, when I went walking alone, I would spend the entire time ruminating, fantasizing about what I should have done instead, or dreaming about some idealized future. None of that helped me settle. A hard, sweaty yoga practice, however, did. It cleared out enough anxiety and worry that I could settle in and listen afterward.

Use who you are and what your body needs to support you. This phase never has to mean being stationary or sitting on a meditation cushion. If you need movement to get your bother on, then get moving. It might look like trying something new or more challenging, which I did when I learned to run. That kind of movement can give you renewed confidence, improve your mood, and make it easier to be with yourself. If you read this section on settling and get fidgety and keep staying busy, take a walk or put on music and move *all the while staying in touch with your intention to settle*. Keep bringing your mind and body back to the discipline of being, which can be such a liberating practice.

Not Your Circus, Not Your Monkeys

Our *why bother* is always connected to other people. You may bother about the climate crisis or species going extinct, or about the people you want to advocate for, or you may care that your children have a rich life filled with love. But if you do not acknowledge what's in it for you, if you refuse to get clear on why you want to care, you are likely to careen back to being resentful and burned out.

When we aren't settling in and listening patiently, our strength of connection can turn against us, meaning we prioritize caring for others over caring for ourselves, or that we use caring for others as a reason not to take the space we need to find our desire. It can become an excuse to never settle into ourselves and find the life we want to live, and it can lead to higher rates of anxiety and depression.

My friend Kristina contracted pneumonia every year after Christmas for three or four years, becoming bedridden for weeks. She finally learned to say no to her in-laws and her own extended family's holiday demands, as well as to her internalized image of what a meaningful holiday looked like. The funny thing was when she was sick, she got all the settling and resting she needed. She would reemerge each time clearer on what she bothered about, which at the time was painting and building her business.

There is an inherent healthy selfishness to bothering again. This selfishness, when acknowledged and protected with healthy boundaries, makes it possible to find your desire. I was in a discussion about this on social media, asking what people's experiences had been with making space for desire to show up, and Barb, a reader and student, sent me this story: "I was five years into the chaos of my son's addiction and all the accompanying trauma. I was feeling epically depleted, having put every ounce of my energy into trying to save him. I feared he would die. At a women's retreat, I talked about this. Another mom said, 'We're only as happy as our unhappiest child.' Every fiber of my being revolted with a whole-body visceral 'NO!' That would *not* be my truth. I began to redefine what a 'good mother' is and what 'love' means and does. I gave myself permission to have peace and joy in my life, permission to live my life fully, no matter what was going on with my son. I realized that it is possible to love and let go simultaneously. And the first strong nudge toward my work to support moms impacted by a child's addiction and other mental health conditions came to me."

Barb found a way to flourish even as her son struggled with drug addiction, while Catharine found freedom to rediscover desire while being the sole caretaker of her mother, someone who "managed to suck the creative oxygen out of air. I reached a point where I thought, 'Never mind.' The only women who could create something new in their fifties were women who were free of their mothers— and I was *not* free of mine. The fairy tales of the child who can act on the call for adventure only after her mother dies?

I thought, 'When I am finally free for an adventure, I will be too old.' I was struggling with how to set boundaries so I could create. I took a class in poetry. And I started journaling more, working to isolate what exactly it was that held me back and how life could be better if I took steps down new paths. I took weekend getaways that didn't include Mom and risked making bigger, scarier, crazier art. Because there is no more time, I cannot wait for the moment of release. I must find the way now before it's too late."

When my mom was in the early stages of Alzheimer's, but we didn't know it yet, and she was an alcoholic, she would invade our home. She would regularly drive up the driveway, barge into our house in the middle of the workday, demanding Bob or I stop work and spend time with her. Once I had to lock myself in my bathroom to finish a client call. Bob and I talked to her, we drew healthy boundaries, and she rode right over them. We locked the front door and ignored her. The day she got her diagnosis, I asked the neurologist, "Can Mom still drive?"

He blanched. "Absolutely not. Your mom has almost no spatial awareness now. She can't drive again." This was the most devastating news for Mom, far more than losing her mind and eventually her life. But for me? It was a reprieve from being invaded. I'd never have to hear her car grinding over the fat cement lip of my driveway again. That's not a pretty story, but it's a true one. The cost of having our own lives can be astronomical.

Then reality set in. My sister lived across the country in Florida. I would be Mom's primary caregiver. I was emerging from the black hole that had me wanting to slip over the edge of the ferry. Lilly had recently started at the University of Washington, and as much as I missed her, it was wonderful to feel freer. Bob and I would marry in less than a year. I was planning to bravely ask and wait to hear what was next for me. But now I would have to care for my mom? I was furious.

Ah, what a noble reason to hide behind: caretaking. Running over every morning to make sure she took her various medications. Driving her to the senior center where she still wanted to volunteer, not realizing she was now one of "them." Patiently taking her to the dentist and doctor. Finding people to help her around the house and take her shopping, her favorite activity. I'd get patted on the back for being a good daughter and I could shove my questions of what to bother about away. No sitting in stillness for me.

Mom's lack of boundaries became mine, her ten phone calls a day my excuse to leave myself. When her friend, whom we hired to take her shopping and out to lunch once a week, let her get drunk at lunch and dropped her off at our house and drove away, I secretly loved the drama. I discovered a remarkable ability to morph into a martyr, to bustle about with a slightly aggrieved smile plastered on my face, while escalating the level of caretaking far past what she needed.

It took me most of the next two years to understand my guilt for judging my mom was driving the busywork. I wasn't settling down and accepting my feelings or my reality; I was running as fast as I could and giving myself plenty to do so I couldn't stop.

My family finally alerted me that my martyrdom was in fact endangering Mom. "Jennifer, she can't remember how to close the bread bag," my sister Michele said, mimicking our mom fumbling with the hard-plastic clip. "She can't live by herself any longer." I had been so busy doing that I hadn't noticed how far her disease had progressed.

A beautiful new assisted living and memory care facility was being built four blocks from my house. For the two months before they opened, I tried to convince Mom how awesome it would be to live there. I hoped she would be less lonely, that the activities and other people struggling with age and memory issues could fill her days. I finally, gingerly welcomed my grief and judgment. I grieved that I would never have the mom I wanted, and that I'd never appreciated the mom I had. I grieved the loss of my dad, and the family I had with my first husband. I saw it was time to be grateful and embrace the family I was making with Bob, and then I had to grieve how I had held myself back from doing just that. I had never sat still long enough to grieve all that happened in the past few years: death, divorce, illness, and failing to be fully present in loving Bob.

When I finally got around to doing the work of grieving and of *feeling*, I didn't do so quickly or neatly. I came around to how to bother in loops and backflips. Grief has no expiration date but, bit by bit, mine no longer came trailing regret and resignation and self-hatred. I learned to grieve in a way that helps me bother, that opens me up instead of closing me down. How? I wrote about my relationship with my mom, and in doing so, I understood my mom had been happy. She'd treasured her life of entertaining, playing tennis, and making quilts from kits. She'd loved being admired for her beauty and style. Yes, she was also unhappy. She hadn't known how to find her *why bother* after my sister and I had grown up and moved away. Her drinking became a way to mask her unexplored desires. But that wasn't my fault, and it wasn't my problem to fix.

Mom could no longer read, drive, speak more than a few sentences without aphasia eating her words, or find her way from the dining room back to her room. After Mom had been in the facility for a few months, Judith, the activity director, ran into me in the hallway. Judith was an athletic, energetic woman in her late fifties. She said, "Jennifer, your mother needs a purpose. She needs a purpose in life. That's why she's so depressed."

I gazed at her, excited to hear her plan to give my mom a reason to bother. And then I got it: Judith wanted me to find a purpose for my mom. All I got out was "I so agree with you," then stumbled down the windowless hallway and out the glass double doors into the blinding afternoon. I walked home. I could walk. I could walk home. Or I could turn the other way and walk into town, buy something in a store, get books out of the library, whatever I wanted. Or I could drive anywhere I wanted. I took in the cracks in the sidewalk, the shaggy Christmas tree farm between Mom's place and our neighborhood, the slight hill I was climbing and the delightful effort it took to climb it.

I walked into the truth I had been dodging: I was the only one who could live my *why bother*. I couldn't save my mom and she had never asked me to. It was as stark as the spring light. I would no longer squander, I would no longer hide.

What seems to put many people off about having boundaries is it can feel like pitting what you want against what someone needs. It also isn't helpful to judge the people you need space from for being so needy, because it keeps the focus on them instead of you. Try creating boundaries as a pause, a break, a way to make space for desire to show itself. Then it's less about what you are denying someone else or about judging them, and more about what is drawing you forward. Or perhaps, like me, you will need to turn your story that you must sacrifice yourself for someone else inside out and explore where you might be hiding from desire by over-caretaking others. Whatever your approach, don't judge yourself as wrong for caring and being in relationship, and don't make it okay to sacrifice your *what's next* for someone else's comfort.

Reflect

What helps you settle? Perhaps doing something that tires your body or being with others in ritual, like a worship service or shared meditation. Does it help to set a clear intention, put your phone in the drawer, turn off the computer?

What might you need to wean yourself off by saying no? You don't have to know what's next to say no now. You are making space to settle, space for what's next to show itself.

What pulls you back into doing, especially those things that you no longer want to bother about? What scatters your energy and makes you feel the day has been a waste?

What keeps convincing you "just this one time" and then you regret the choice?

Who, if anyone, voices worries and fears about when you will get into action or figure things out? Perhaps rehearse a line or two to deflect their concern. For example, "Thanks for asking. But tell me, what are you up to these days?" Or draw a boundary about how much time you spend with them, for now.

What will never become clear, never sink in, never be possible if you don't settle?

Who or what will you allow to steal your future?

Without desire, there is no life.

---

(8)

Desire

You've been creating the conditions for desire to flourish: a settled mind and calm body, the alert courage that comes from self-compassionate grit and trust in yourself and the creative process. All that you've been reflecting on so far creates the space for longing and possibility to show itself, and for you to stay patiently open and present with desire while it unfolds.

To know desire gives you energy, pleasure, connection, and direction. When encountered with consciousness, desire becomes an express lane to becoming more truly yourself. Desire can look so simple—using your best dishes every day or deciding you deserve clothes that make you feel good now, not when you lose weight. Desire can change the course of your life forever—you could foster a kid, sell your belongings and sail around the world, come out as non-binary to your evangelical church. Desire is what brought you into life. It's what brings love into form. It's what keeps us growing past what we know.

I've been trying to understand desire for decades. I've denied it, short-changed it, ignored it, but I've learned that without desire, there is no life. There are simulations, approximations, imitations, and that's sometimes enough—until it isn't.

Desire can feel hot, all-consuming, too much to bear. You want to possess the object of your desire, hold on to it, merge with it. I feel that face of desire when I want to get closer to Bob but I don't know how, or when I'm tired from working and instead of giving myself the kindness I want, like a nap or a walk or time to read a novel, I gobble half a bag of popcorn while reading the news.

When I was younger, this grabby kind of desire was about *getting*—if I could get a successful screenwriting career, if I could get slimmer, if I could get a cute apartment near the beach, then I would be who I desired. I treated my desires as something to fulfill, to arrive at, not as a way to come alive or to learn what mattered most to me. I could rarely stand long in the sensation of wanting. I knew desire as a consumer, as way to get something.

The kind of desire you want to know is not about consuming. It is about power, sovereignty, pleasure, joy, self-expression, living truthfully, and allowing the pulse of life to live through you. It's knowing what you want so you can choose what to do with your time, energy, and resources, as much as you are able. Desire is thus tied to privilege and to self-regard. We can't talk about the desires of women, of men who don't or won't fit inside the accepted power structures, or of genderqueer folks without looking at the oppression and violence against our desires, the freedom denied to so many for so long, the freedom to even name a desire, let alone act on it. We're allowed to want but only within certain parameters that make us useful, productive, attractive, pleasing, or at the very least controlled, living within prescribed lines.

Roxane Gay's memoir *Hunger* is one story of desire turned against oneself. She was gang-raped by neighborhood boys when she was twelve, and to keep herself safe, over the years, she gained weight. At one point, she weighed 577 pounds at six foot three. "My body is wildly undisciplined," Gay writes,

> and yet I deny myself nearly everything I desire. I deny myself the right to space when I am in public, trying to fold in on myself, to make my body invisible even though it is in fact grandly visible. I deny myself the right to a shared armrest because how dare I impose? I deny myself entry into certain spaces I have deemed inappropriate for a body like mine—most spaces inhabited by other people, public transportation, anywhere I could be seen or where I might

be in the way, really. I deny myself bright colors in my daily
clothing choices, sticking to a uniform of denim and dark
shirts even though I have a far more diverse wardrobe...
How dare I confess my want? How dare I try to act on that
want? I deny myself so much, and still there is much desire
throbbing beneath my surfaces.

Gay is not extreme in her denial or reaction, not at all. If it's
not food we deny ourselves (understandable in our body-
shaming, fat-fearful world), it's asking for what we want
during sex or negotiating for a raise or expressing ourselves
creatively. Michelle wrote to me, "I eat my favorite flavor of
Skittles last. When I want things, I save them for last... I can't
let myself consume what I want." But Anne eats her favorite
foods first and quickly, unable to enjoy the tastes and textures,
because she fears they might be taken away from her as they
were when she was a child.

Desire is hard for anyone who doesn't fit the straight white
cis male mold—and even for people who do. I have watched
both my husbands—white straight guys—struggle mightily to
name and then ask for what they want in an intimate relationship. Desire gets tangled in shame for most of us, thanks to
so many confusing messages from religion, commerce, culture. Yet even so, I believe women have a much more difficult
time claiming what they want. I only have to look at the stories I grew up reading like *Madame Bovary*, *Anna Karenina*,
The House of Mirth, "The Yellow Wallpaper," *Beloved*. I never

thought twice about the fact that every heroine in these books killed herself because she had no option to create the life she wanted. But when I watched *Thelma & Louise* in 1991, I did think twice. I left the movie theater shaking, thinking, "How could they die? Could the writer think that was the only option?" It's nearly thirty years later and life has changed for most of us in terms of our options, and yet desire remains a dicey frontier. To desire is to be vulnerable, to risk heartbreak, and to risk life. To desire often requires transgressing against the lessons of your childhood, your past, your roles, and facing down the ways your culture, your job, and your community does and doesn't support you.

Pam wrote me a beautiful letter about why she is afraid to desire: "Expressing a desire or even a true physical need was dangerous when I was a child. Expressing a desire was to draw attention to myself... Better to be silent and forgotten. I learned never to express desire and this grew into never even admitting desire to myself, lest I slip up and reveal it to someone else." Out of the thousands of women I have worked with in workshops, retreats, and one on one, I would say most of them are frightened or at least apprehensive about knowing what they truly want, let alone taking action on it. I can think of dozens of women and a few men I've worked with who for years have wanted to come out of hiding and claim their writing or their business dreams—it's that common.

Even when we don't learn to overtly hide our desires or fear them, we absorb the messages that wanting something is at best a mixed bag. We might be labeled selfish or a ball-busting bitch or for men, overbearing or selfish. When we want, we know we will have to make hard choices because we can't have it all. Nobody ever could. We might be publicly shamed. And how do we even know what we want? How can we be sure?

My father was raised during the Depression on a small farm in southern Indiana. After serving in World War II, he borrowed $3,200 from his older brother and worked seven days a week for two decades to build a successful business. I was born when Dad was forty-three and on top of his world. He wanted me to have everything he never did. My parents brought me up with a sense of abundance, often telling me, "You can do anything you want," while demonstrating that my dad's desires mattered far more than my mom's. I was caught between believing in myself and doubting my desires were as real as a man's. I spent many decades pinging between bold action and crippling self-doubt, as the larger culture reinforced this contradictory message. Want, but don't want too much or too publicly.

With the rise of social media, desire has become suspect in a whole new way. Is that a real desire I'm seeing or an influencer's desire that's for sale? How dare you have that desire when other people can't, what kind of selfish, insensitive, privileged shithead are you? How can I desire when people are recovering from yet another "unprecedented storm of the century"? How can I desire when my friend's friend is dying from breast cancer? How can my desire matter when the Amazon rainforest is burning?

Clearly, *desire* is a loaded word. Why even go near it? Why not set goals or talk about ambition or use the word *dream* instead?

Because those words are too puny, too mundane for the task. Desire is the best word precisely because of its fraught history. Desire is a one-word feminist manifesto. It says, "This is big stuff you are grappling with and you need to bring all you've got." You *must* relate to desire to get your bother on, and there are three parts to it, or ways in:

1. Self-determination

Feminist psychologist and Jungian analyst Polly Young-Eisendrath notes in *Women and Desire*, "A woman who identifies with being the Object of Desire is not the source of her own inspiration; she does not feel as though her life belongs to her. Her vitality and imagination, her efforts and plans, are directed toward the desires of others, toward being desirable . . . To be the Object of Desire means to have no core self, no clear autonomy and self-determination that are under your command." To have a healthy relationship with desire, you must first believe your life belongs to you, is under your control, and that you have the right to live your life the way you wish—even if someone labels you not nice, pushy, a bitch. To desire is to have the right to choose. When you don't think you're allowed, you end up pretending, pleasing, or giving yourself a halfway kind of desire.

A friend in her mid-thirties fell in love with a charismatic man. He was adamant he did not want children. She had always very much wanted a child. But she decided the relationship was worth closing the door on being a mother. When they broke up ten years later, she realized within months that she had to honor her desire to be a mother. She wrote me, "I just needed to let myself want what I wanted, and try for what my heart desired. I'd done such a good job, all those years with L., of making peace with not being able to have or even try for something that my heart wanted. I think it shut off a lot of other things. I made peace with it, but in the process the deepest, most creative part of me got the message that what I desired was inappropriate or unnecessary. So even if no baby comes from this, just telling my family and friends, 'This is something I want, for no reason other than that I want it,' and to have them line up to support me (I have had five offers of donors from friends, and my parents are supportive too) has been quite overwhelming. It feels like even if nothing more comes of this, I'm healing something." I saved my friend's email and read it from time to time. "For no reason other than that I want it": that's being the subject of your own desires. That's sovereignty.

2. Inspirational foreshadowing

In your preferences, hunches, and most heartfelt longings lives the visible shape of your particular life—what brings you alive and into life. "Desire is evolutionary—it leads to your becoming," writes my friend, author and entrepreneurial mentor Hiro Boga. Mark Epstein concurs in *Open to Desire*: "Desire is the crucible within which the self is formed... When we are out of touch with our desires, we cannot be ourselves... desire is our vitality, an essential component of our human experience, that which gives us our individuality [and] at the same time keeps prodding us out of ourselves." That individuality and vitality is where your *why bother* lives. And in embracing desire, we find the direction that prods us to care and take action in sustainable ways.

3. Spiritual connection

When I can accept the yearnings that will forever throb in me and ease into them without trying to consume something, achieve something, or fix something, desire contains everything I could ever want. In the moment of wanting, when I don't contract around it, there is all of life and I am not separate from it. Or as Sanskrit scholar and author of *The Radiance Sutras* Lorin Roche says, "The ultimate source of desire is the soul's impulse to express itself in the world." In that sensation and sparkle of desire lies all of creation and, for me, the deepest experience of *why bother*, one that propels me to care for students, my family, the planet.

Desire as a word has power and reckoning and juice. Denial of desire lurks in the deadening kind of *why bother*, the kind that brought you to this book. Saying "I want a Cobb salad" doesn't sound life-changing but as I've seen so many times—and each time it makes my heart catch with joy— when someone honestly claims the simplest desire, without hiding or making excuses or settling for less, their world begins to shift.

I don't mean to suggest a healthy life-giving relation- ship with desire is about *getting* what you want. That's nice (I do love a good Cobb salad), but it's not the point. When we relate to desire solely as getting what we want, we nar- row its life-giving power to a trickle. We give disappointment and loss the power to crush us. When we confuse desire with a positive or even perfect outcome and we get frustrated, rejected, and our hearts are hurt—which will happen—we may decide desiring is a fool's game and agree to settle into resignation and resentment. But that is a tragic error. Cling- ing, performing, pleasing, or wanting to preserve your life in amber is not desire. It's your emotional immune system say- ing, "Go back now!" It's the dominant culture saying, "Want these things this way, or don't want at all." Living lies in the doing, not the having.

Desire's purpose is not to get you somewhere or some- thing but to get you *here*. To awaken you to a deeper aliveness, an intimacy like no other. To help you flourish, help you enjoy, to bring you into the pleasurable pulse of life. Desire is the current of the river of "no forcing, no holding back." Life without desire is inconceivable. None of us would exist, for starters, nor would whatever you are sitting on or the roof over your head or the words you are reading.

Everything starts with desire. You can't bother without it. Desire is your power, your path, the energy to persevere. And yet it can feel dangerous, unattainable, tinged with the forbidden. How do you hold both? How do you open to desire without being owned by it? These are very worthy questions we will explore.

Desiring Is a Naked Act

We must be naked with ourselves and accept that we have desires, and we must then accept that it's okay to have these desires, even if we can't precisely name them or fulfill them. Desires can conflict with each other, or we can be terrified of what will happen if we acknowledge them. This is much more difficult to do than most of us realize, as I came to learn when I fell in love with Bob.

Two years before the ferry incident and six months after my first husband and I split up, I met Bob. He was one of those uncommonly great guys who still exist in the world, and he was a grown-up (rather than a man-child): sane, responsible, emotionally available, and willing to risk loving again. When you live on a small island where most everybody is married, finding love is akin to finding perfect jeans in a thrift store for ten bucks. I was flush with luck.

It almost didn't go that way. I blew him off on our first date. We winked at each other on an online dating site, and I agreed to meet for coffee one afternoon before Lilly got home from school. He was also recently separated and shell-shocked from his wife's long decline into mental illness, which he told me about over his Americano and my hot chocolate. He was so nervous he could barely look at me, his eyes darting everywhere but into mine, as he mopped his sweaty forehead with a blue bandanna.

My dating handbook stated, "Thou shalt not talk about one's ex-wife on the first date." Standing on the sidewalk afterward, both of us heading home to meet our kids, I was all about my firm boundaries. "It was fun to hang out, but we clearly don't have a romance here," I said.

He laughed, a self-confident chuckle, which gave me pause. I hadn't taken the wind out of his sails one bit. "I just wanted to get out of the house," he said. "That was the most I've talked to another adult in months. Thanks for listening. Can I hug you goodbye?"

"I'm a heel," I thought, "for being so judgmental." I hugged him. I noticed how snugly I fit under his arm. He was close to a foot taller than me. Still, as I drove around the corner and up the hill to my house, I congratulated myself. I'd told him no! I knew what I wanted: someone without baggage. Someone with a bright future!

Two hours later, he emailed me. He had looked me up online and he complimented my work. He was such a good writer that I read and reread every one of his emails. And he was a devoted dad. Did I mention his swimmer's shoulders or his long powerful legs from playing rugby and now tennis? Or the weird similarities we shared, like both having had a dog named Atticus? Having knee surgery on the same knee by the same surgeon in Santa Barbara only a few years apart? Loving square dancing in seventh grade?

Three weeks later, sitting astride Bob on his couch, half undressed, I blurted out, "I love you."

"I knew it!" Bob said, grabbing me and squeezing me to him. "I knew it!"

I wanted to bolt out the front door, run home, lock my door. I wanted to say, "I didn't mean it! I just wanted to feel close to you." But I snuggled against his broad chest and laughed. Because I loved him and it terrified me. But I wasn't somebody who let herself know she was terrified, so on I careened.

We did fun things, which is something Chris and I had mostly forgotten how to do in the last five years or more of our marriage. We camped at Wenas Creek on the west side of the Cascades where he introduced me to birding. He cooked for me: spaghetti with spicy tomato sauce, "boiled dinner" (corned beef and root vegetables), Copper River salmon with greens from the farmers market. We climbed up to the bow of the ferry and posed like Rose and Jack in *Titanic*, even though neither of us had seen the movie because we thought it would be too sad. He read my books, and when I protested, "Don't read those. I will write the book I was really meant to write," he shushed me.

"Your books are great. *The Comfort Queen's Guide to Life* is my favorite, but I love them all. You change women's lives."

We introduced our kids to each other at the Indian restaurant above the movie theater. Aidan was three years younger than Lilly and he exclaimed, "She can't sit next to me!" when Bob started to slide in next to me in the booth. But after the movie he skipped his lanky body alongside Lilly's on the way to the car, chattering about the special effects and asking her what her favorite part was. Lilly gave her approval of Aidan— "He's cute"—but held Bob at arm's length for years to come. Bob shrugged and said, "I could never replace her dad and I would never try."

I laughed when we made love, laughed when I had an orgasm. "I used to cry," I thought one day in the shower. "Now I laugh."

To the world, I was a successful post-divorce story, the picture of resilience. I got into great shape and felt terrific. I was in a loving relationship. Our kids liked each other. My publisher was releasing my latest book in paperback to give it a second life. I designed a new online course, tied to the book's release, encompassing many of my best ideas for living a life of creativity and agency. It was 2008. The economy was in a terrifying free fall, but Bob and I moved into my house together, which meant we cut our expenses in half. I had health benefits as his "domestic partner," so I was much safer financially than I'd been for years.

Still, I couldn't shake the feeling that I wasn't allowed to have all this—it was too much goodness and too soon. I was missing something and as soon as I remembered it, everything would come crashing down.

One night, in bed, the summer twilight still bright enough that I could see Bob, I lifted my head from his chest and asked him, "I can really have this, can't I?" He gently guided my head back to rest on him.

"You can, baby, of course, you can." I listened to his heartbeat and tried to believe him.

We'd said early on neither of us wanted to marry again. It felt unnecessary, a developmental stage we'd both moved through. Even more so, for me, I never wanted to marry again because I never wanted the state to have a say in my life. When you divorce in Washington State, you have to go before a judge. I had stood before mine, a woman with a perfectly blow-dried pageboy who frowned at me with what I imagined was disdain and asked, "Are you pregnant?" and "Are there any other adults living in your home with you and your daughter?" I almost mouthed off, but my lawyer shot me a stern look and I answered meekly, "No. No." Other people waited behind me for their turn to be grilled. I felt like a criminal, and I walked out of the courthouse into the chilly morning like they had acquitted me of a crime I had committed. I almost sprinted to my Honda. I called Bob, who was at out of town at a meeting. "It was so awful."

"Oh, baby, I should have been there with you." I shook my head. I was glad I was alone. I wanted no one ever to know what happened. I wanted to forget that courtroom as fast as I could.

"I never ever want to do that again."

"We won't sweetie, we'll never do that to each other."

I drove home and took a long hot shower.

But since we are being honest here, there was another reason I never wanted to get married again: because it would be easier for me to leave.

Even as Bob became my family, my tether to the world and I his, a part of me fantasized about being alone. Off in a small cottage, far from neighbors, hidden beneath tall Douglas firs. Lilly would be there, but we fit into each other's aloneness perfectly. When she went away to college in three years, I'd tuck away, waiting for her visits. Alone. Reading, walking the dogs, seeing friends, writing novels. That would be my life. There would be people and yet I would be alone. I savored my fantasy of aloneness like a prisoner might a fantasy of an escape tunnel. Come to think of it, and you probably already did: I savored it like I would my future ferry fantasy.

When Bob asked me to tell him what I wanted during sex or to stay present when we disagreed or to thaw when I turned into an ice woman after we fought, I couldn't. I wanted to, but I still froze. I sensed something wasn't kosher about this habit of mine. Maybe I had done something similar in my marriage to Chris and that's why we hadn't made it? "Nah," I told myself, "that wasn't it." Chris couldn't grow up; he'd had a midlife crisis after his recovery from cancer and he'd left me. And when he'd come back a few months later, I hadn't been willing to try again. I'd cut and run. Selfish but also smart. Anyway, I was made to be alone. I needed to be alone. You can't change a tiger's stripes and all that.

But then Bob would draw me back to him with his steadiness and his whole-hearted vulnerability, and I was all in. Then he would get too close with his "I love you so much" or something else would trigger me, and off I would emotionally scamper. I wanted to believe the rainbow and unicorn story of our midlife love—we had lived three miles away from each on the same island for all those years—but the part of me that didn't think I deserved all this was getting squirrelly.

How could all this goodness not save me from the spreading numbness, the low thud of *why bother*, that was taking over my life? How could Bob, my daughter, and my bonus boy, Aidan, not give me the juice to keep going? The neuroscience geek in me wants to talk about hedonic adaptation, the tendency for us to return to our happiness set point after a positive or negative change. Which means my brain went back to its pre-Bob, post-divorce, post-Dad's-death funk. The ontological coach in me wants to point out there was a lot of unfinished business about my divorce, how I handled Dad's death, and a pile of other regrets demanding my attention.

All true, but what really mattered, the writer in me thinks, is I didn't believe the new story unfolding—that someone could love me as I was, which, it turns out, is one of my deepest and most terrifying desires.

I never told Bob about my ferry-jumping fantasy until I was writing this chapter, and then only in passing, as we both did our evening chores. He was marinating chicken in his famous miso sauce, I was feeding the dogs, maneuvering around each other in the long narrow space between our kitchen island and counter.

"I mean, I would have never done it," I said, putting the bowls of kibble down. "Not in a million years." I knew he might be angry. I kept moving, putting away the clean dishes from the dishwasher. I could feel Bob looking at me, but I kept tidying. When in doubt, keep moving.

"Wait, this was after we met?" he finally said, facing me, the pan of chicken in his hands.

Damn, I had hoped he wouldn't put the timeline together. "Yep, but c'mon, we both had a big dip after the initial falling in love phase. You had to reckon with bad stuff too." I didn't want to remind him of his own descent into depression, the aftereffects of his ex-wife's mental illness. We had both struggled.

I attacked the mail pile, sorting recycling from bills. He put the chicken in the oven. "I guess," he said. "But that's not the way I remember it. I remember being so happy."

I wanted to hug him and say, "I'm sorry it took me so long to get with the program. I'm sorry I hid from you," but I wasn't

brave enough. I changed the subject to buying airline tickets for our kids' next Colorado visit. Later, when we were in
bed, my head once again on his chest, I found the courage to
explain how hard it was to let him love me. But as I stumbled
over my words, tried to talk about desire and being afraid of
what I wanted, about intimacy and being accepted by him, it
occurred to me: he knew all that long before I did.

I know he knew because Bob got me to choose love. To be
seen as I was. To allow my deepest desire to be acknowledged.
It started—and almost ended—on a trip to Guatemala. Bob
loves to travel, especially in Latin America where he lived and
worked for years, and he gets antsy and unhappy if we don't
make room in our lives for regular adventures. He'd found
a week-long yoga and meditation retreat for us, followed by
five days of travel.

The retreat was at a yoga center perched on the rim of Lake
Atitlán. We did an early morning meditation practice, walking down the steep hill from our casita through the tropical
reds and yellows and the smell of mangos to the airy meditation hall. I followed my breath while, in the background,
pangas tut-tutted across the lake, taking Mayan villagers to
work in Panajachel and kids to school. Our retreat leaders
were a married couple, Patricia and Surya, both willowy and
loving. I relaxed completely into the sweet, wide calm I so
loved about being on retreat.

Which made it even more jolting when my old "you need
to be alone, you only deserve to be alone" story grabbed me.
We had met Lynda, who had come on the retreat by herself,

and one day, during free time, she offered to show Bob and me her room. The retreat center had been built up over years and each room was unique, decorated with tile murals of Ganesh and local textiles, views of the lake and the three volcanoes, each like a child's drawing in their iconic shape. Lynda's room was at the top of the three-story building.

I stood in the middle of her room, Bob behind me, a breeze ruffling the muslin curtains, and I thought, "She's alone. She's all alone here." By dinner, I was scheming: how would I get Bob and Aidan to move back into their house, get rid of their tenants? Or I could convince Bob to sell his house and buy the house next door to mine, which was for sale. We'd be close, we'd be together, but not *too* close. During meditation practice that night, instead of concentrating on the mantras, I replayed my fantasy of aloneness. It was both comforting and horrible, like picking a scab.

After practice, Patricia announced we'd be going into silence in the morning, a day early, and we'd stay silent a day longer than originally planned. "Oh goodie," I thought. Being in silence was almost as good as being alone. I didn't even have to make eye contact.

Bob had missed the evening session because he was queasy, and when I went back to our room and told him about the change in plans, he sat up in bed and almost shouted, "But that means we'll be silent on Valentine's Day!"

I was in the small kitchen, getting my vitamins. I kept my face turned away from him and thought, "The man can't be quiet. This is why I need to be alone." Always so convenient to blame someone else for our unseen desires.

After meditation on the second day, we broke silence. Everyone was chatty, as if our unused words had to get out and fast. Dinner was louder and more animated than usual. You would have thought we were all a little drunk, but there was nothing besides guava juice and purified water to drink. Even our serene teachers were voluble, telling stories about how the lake had changed in the years they'd been visiting, rich expats building ornate villas, the increase in backpackers trekking through. But Bob was almost silent, picking at his dinner, running his hand over his goatee.

I went out on the small veranda to talk to two other women but after a few minutes, Bob came out and hovered. "I want to go upstairs," he finally said. I sighed. It wasn't even eight o'clock, we weren't eighty! But I followed him out into the courtyard. "We should get a blanket, lie by the lake, and watch the stars come out," I said.

He shook his head. "I want to show you something in our room." He put his hand on the small of my back and steered me up the steep stairs ahead of him, my skirt brushing the tropical plants I couldn't name. I wanted to go back into silence. I wanted to be alone.

A small worn wooden deck jutted the length of our casita, offering a partial view of the lake. Bob pulled me onto the deck when I started to unlock our front door. "Let's sit out here for a little while."

"But you said you had something to show me?"

He didn't respond, instead he brushed off the chairs at the little table, his nervous kindness annoying me. I pictured myself in Lynda's room, by myself. Bob produced a bar of our favorite chocolate. Sea salt and almond.

"Where did you get this?" I yanked it toward me, snapped off a fat row. "You had this with you the whole time and didn't tell me?" I chewed. A sugar rush: almost as good as the promise of being alone.

"I brought it from home." I pushed the chocolate toward him, but he didn't touch it. He was twisting his hands around something in his lap. I crammed another square in my mouth.

"You don't want any?"

He shook his head. He fumbled in his lap again. He wasn't meeting my eye. I swallowed, the chocolate almost choking me. Someone in the dining hall below us laughed, a high jingly laugh. Bob was sweating. He started talking, but I couldn't hear him, not at first. Because he had placed a box on the table. A ring box. He recited a poem, stumbled, started again.

"'The minute I heard my first love story, I started looking for you / Not knowing how blind I was. Lovers don't just meet somewhere / They're in each other all along.' That's Rumi." I tried to focus on his words. "Last year, when I was looking for something to write on your birthday card, I found this poem and I knew then that I wanted to marry you because I want everyone to know how much I love you. I want everyone to know." He was crying. Often when he cried, I grew cold, like an evil superhero had frozen me in place. He wiped his eyes with the bandanna from his pocket. "Because it's like that for us, like the poem. We've loved each other forever."

He had known since November and he had said nothing. How did he keep that a secret? I had kept the poem pinned on my bulletin board where I saw it every day.

I leaned back. The weather-beaten chair creaked ominously. I popped forward. Bob opened the ring box, took out a braided silver ring. "I have to see if it fits." He slipped the ring on my left hand. It fit perfectly. I stared at the twined silver band. It looked so happy, a happy whole lovely ring. I held out my hand and the ring gleamed back at me.

"Jennifer, will you marry me?"

I rocked back and forth. Looked at the ring instead of Bob.

"It's inscribed," he said, "with the end of the Rumi quote. I found a ring of yours, you only had one, and it was so tiny I thought it had to be a baby ring but that's all I had to go on. I'm so relieved it was the right size." He mopped his forehead. "Baby?" he said, "Are you okay? Say something."

I opened my mouth. There was nothing in my head but noise. "But I'll be next door," I thought, "or you will be at your house and we will spend the weekends together. I'm not fit to be married." Sweat beaded under my breasts. A silence, a different kind of silence than the silence of our retreat, spilled out between us. This was a formality for him, his asking me. A romantic surprise. He had been nervous but also fully expecting me to say, "Of course. Yes!" I had always said he should ask me in some stunning way because Chris hadn't done that. I wanted to be asked. You'll notice the discrepancy right away: I said I never wanted to be married again and I said I wanted him to ask me in some thrilling way. Which was it? Oh, the insistent truth of desire, popping up no matter how hard we try to deny her. It wasn't about getting married or not. It was about a fierce commitment to letting myself be seen no matter what. That's what I kept denying, then flirting with. My real fear had nothing to do with standing in a courtroom again.

"It's okay," Bob said. "We don't have to do it. This was a stupid idea." He pulled the ring box back into his lap.

I got out of my way long enough to grab his hand and mutter something about how romantic he was. How I was caught off guard. Then a shit bomb plopped out of my mouth and onto the table between us. "I love you. I just need to grow into my yes." I darted a look at him. I saw he knew I might fuck this up and I saw him resolve to not let me take him down, not let me break his heart, if that was where I insisted on going.

"Do you want me to put your ring away?" he asked.

"No!" I startled myself with my vehemence. "I want to wear it."

We got ready for bed in silence, politely handing each other the toothpaste, the water bottle to rinse with. "Goodnight," he said, rolling over without hugging me.

I stared up at the brick ceiling, shaped like a beehive, and played with the shiny ring on my finger.

"Whenever a wanting
moment comes,
Celebrate the rising of desire.
Attend to desire itself,
As a shimmering
impulse of energy
Vibrating the body into motion.
In a flash of knowing,
When intelligence arises,
Attend to this rising
As the illumination of the Self."

———————

LORIN ROCHE, THE RADIANCE SUTRAS

The next morning, we were exaggeratedly kind with each other, all "thank you" and "no, after you." Neither one of us brought up the proposal, but it was there, between us, waiting. I kept sneaking glances at my ring. It was so new and perfect. We left the retreat and headed to the market town of Chichicastenango for a night.

In Chichi, Bob kept asking me what I wanted to do. I kept shrugging and then we'd wander the market, me seeking something down the next aisle of handcrafts and food stalls I couldn't name. I wanted something, but what was it? The market was impossible to take in: spicy copal scent, the susurration of Mayan, fried meat, piles of different chilies as high as my chest. And, most of all, the color. The color of the women's clothing, each village represented by a different pattern, the color of the masks, the belts, the blankets, the carvings, the bedspreads, the scarves, the flowers, the sky.

We stood in front of the cathedral to watch a small band of Mayan men perform a ritual at the top of the steep worn marble steps. They had built the church over a Mayan temple and each step, I'd read, represented one month on the Mayan calendar. The men took turns dancing while twirling a large metal wheel studded with lit candles while the other men threw lit firecrackers at their feet and chanted. I kept waiting for someone to get his fingers blown off or for some wild magic to happen, an appearance of spirits or for me to wake up and know what I wanted, to emerge from my shambling blankness. I wanted to hold Bob's hand because I was feeling

less and less substantial, but I didn't. We hadn't touched since
he proposed.

I suddenly had to sleep. Bob turned with me like he was
my shadow.

Outside our colonial hotel, a Cofradia came toward us
on the narrow cobblestoned street. The men wore a uniform
of black short pants and ponchos, with black straw hats that
sat high on their heads atop intricately embroidered scarves.
They were chanting, shaking rattles and beating drums.
Several of the men carried staffs topped with metal suns
and crosses. The heat made the music seem heavy, louder.
I wanted to follow them. Then two men carrying an open-
fronted box across their shoulders drew toward us. I shrank
back, certain the box contained a shriveled corpse, but then I
saw it was a life-sized doll, one of the Catholic saints, I didn't
know which one. Bob pulled me back into a doorway, out of
the way. One man spun away from the procession and loomed
in front of us, locked eyes with me. I stared back. His eyes
were unfocused, almost cloudy. I leaned toward him, wanting
to know what he knew. Bob pressed coins into the man's hand
and he marched away with the group, their drums fading.

I washed my hands and face, slipped off my clothes, and
lay down on one of the double beds. The mattress was thin
and hard, held up by ropes. I knew I should say something: "I
will marry you," or at least "I'm sorry," but I was too sleepy.
Bob settled himself on the other bed and studied a map. I
wanted to explain my need to be alone. I wanted to say, "But

you have done things wrong too; you aren't perfect. It's not just me. You got mad at Lilly that time. And what about your anger? So big and sudden, it filled the house, terrified me. Did you notice the sparring about our kids, the subtle power plays between us about which of ours kid is the best?" Maybe it was mostly my game.

I sighed, rolled over. Bob neatly folded his map, slipped on his shoes. "I'm going out."

"Where?" I looked everywhere but at him. "Don't go. I'll miss you."

He looked at me, his mouth worked like he wanted to say something, then shook his head. "Rest." I watched him leave, his broad shoulders slightly rounded.

From outside, he turned the lock. Always taking care of me.

I was wide awake. Copal smoke drifted inside the open window. I turned over on the hard mattress and stared at the blue sky. Somewhere a drum beat steady and slow.

On the way home to Washington, we had a long layover in Dallas, and Bob had booked us a room in an airport hotel that offered half-day rates. As we checked in at the fancy desk surrounded by well-dressed business travelers and women with big hair, I realized he'd booked the room because he thought we would celebrate our engagement. Having layover sex.

Instead, we washed our hands, I brushed my hair, and we hurried downstairs to eat a nearly silent lunch. The room was too bright, the waiter too chatty, the food tasted synthetic. Back in our room, we lay side by side not talking, not napping, not reading, and not having sex. There was a giant automated blind that, when it was up, allowed you to watch the planes land and take off. Bob closed it and we lay in the expensive, dim quiet until it was time to get up for our plane home.

He was across the room, tying his shoes, when he broke our silence. "What will you tell Lilly?"

I stammered, "I hadn't thought about it."

Bob gave a firm tug to his lace and then looked up at me. His eyes were red. "Look, I don't want to tell the kids." He struggled to keep his voice steady. "Nothing has to change." He looked down at his shoes. "Let's pretend I never asked. I don't want anyone to know I asked you, okay?"

In front of me, two paths showed themselves. I was still in the fancy hotel room with the big window looking out over the runways. Bob was there, rubbing his hand across his head like he could smooth away his sadness and, stretching out as if drawn on the hotel carpet, were two visible choices. One was the life I would live alone. Hiding my ugly self away from everyone. Hiding from Bob, hiding from Lilly. Hiding. I saw my cottage under big trees, covered in vines and surrounded by a wildflower garden. It was a fairy-tale cottage, constructed from childhood books, and it was empty. Empty of energy, of motion, of life. But oh, was it appealing. I wanted that cottage, that emptiness. I wanted to hide.

The other path I had never seen before. It was not one my mind had conjured a thousand times before. It had shape but nothing else. It was brightness. The path itself blazed and disappeared into lightness. There was no image of the end, only a fizzy daring *yes*.

Each path stretched in front of me. I understood I had a choice. It was actually up to me which path I chose. I wasn't destined for the empty pretty cottage unless I wanted to be. I never understood this before—that I could choose. That it was an act of desire and self-regard to choose.

A thought or a voice asked, "Could it be this easy?" My body answered yes, completely yes. It could be this easy. I could have what I wanted. I looked at Bob and imagined that I said no and he eventually left me, because he got tired of me running away.

But he was here, tucking in his shirt. I inhaled and yelled, "Okay!"

Bob peered across the room at me as if across a canyon. "Okay, what?" The tentativeness in his tone made me cringe.

"Okay, I will marry you!" I yelled.

The air between us vibrated as we stared at each other. The sad heaviness he had been trying to hide since he had asked me peeled away from his usually open and trusting face.

"Really, okay?" he asked.

That stung, but as I crossed the room and grabbed him, I thought he had every right to doubt me. I would have to earn his trust. And my own.

"More than okay."

We kissed. I will remember that kiss for the rest of my life.

I needed to learn how to give myself permission to desire, and doing that in the presence of someone else was, for me, the key. By making a commitment to Bob, by committing to not hiding from him any longer, I began to get my bother on in that moment. I stopped running, dithering, and denying what I wanted.

Desire rarely accords with the sanitized, pretty version I want to hold of myself. The feminist in me cringes that deciding to marry a man was my turning point. But we are shaped by a thousand factors outside our awareness and control. Desiring is an act of transgression against outer rules and an act of transgression against our inner rules and our story about who we are.

When I asked readers to tell me about how they desired, Lora wrote, "Sometimes, it seems I only sip at my desire, to make it last as long as possible. When perhaps there is an endless bounty and I could shower myself, and there would still be plenty." While Margie said, "I have a love/hate relationship with desire. It can quicken and delight... and can also be a monster in my belly that says 'Feed me' with a gaping mouth. The level of control and balance I have determines which side I experience."

Caroline Knapp writes about women finding fulfillment of their desires in *Appetites*: "The key—the bridge to the shore—is agency, a feeling (almost always hard-won) that marries entitlement with power: I *deserve* to be filled becomes I *can* be filled. I can make it happen."

Few of us get to ask "What do I want?" on a regular unconstrained basis, given life's demands and petty details (like making a living) but—and this is a very important but—the most common way we cut desire off is by telling ourselves,

"Why bother to even ask?" We confuse getting what we want with feeling life flowing through us. You can't do that anymore.

You've prepared the way for desire to flow. Repeat after me: it's safe to desire. Say it aloud. *It's safe to desire.*

What do you feel when you say, "It's safe to desire"? Fear, panic, unease? Or hell yes! Does it trigger a memory of being told how ungrateful you are for wanting, or "good luck with that, as if that could happen for me"? Anger as in, "How the hell do you know if it's safe for me to desire?" Excitement as in, "Well, what's next?" A sudden need to text your partner, your kid, to make sure they're okay? Or all of the above?

Substitute Desires

Why do we settle for substitutes? Because fulfilling our true desire is hard work! The world sells desire as a glossy state of ideal feeling, as goddess-infused crystal-encrusted self-care, as rainbow-hued self-fulfillment and glowing happiness, a Marie Kondo sock drawer, a wrinkle-free brow.

My experience of desire is nothing like that. It's far more unruly, primitive, intense, plugging my power cord into the cosmos's electrical socket. And it's work. It's not about how I want to feel; it's about what has to be felt so life can flow through me.

We settle for substitutes because we haven't learned how to have a healthy relationship with desire, because we've been shamed or punished for having desires, because desire can feel so big. There's nothing wrong with giving ourselves substitutes sometimes, but if that's all we ever give ourselves? Then life becomes one dreary, dull, *why bother* snore.

Time monsters, like shadow comforts, are substitute desires. They are things you have to do in life and some-times even want to do—laundry, email, paying bills, cleaning the bathtub, volunteering, bringing soup to a sick friend—but they become activities that eat your time when you are dodging or afraid to give yourself what you truly want. When I spend ten minutes in the morning checking email and answering quick questions from clients, and then I write, I am managing my responsibilities and putting my mind at ease so I can concentrate. When I answer all my email; check the Oasis group online; check in with the Brain Trust, my peer mastermind group; or read a student's work before I write—even though I enjoy all these activities—I am feeding my time monsters.

It's not about eliminating shadow comforts or time mon-sters entirely—that's impossible. That pits your weaker conscious control against your much faster and emotionally charged unconscious and that can easily slide into a moral judgment. Abstain and you're a good person; give in and you're weak. Everybody needs comfort and downtime, espe-cially when you are starting to bother again because it can be hard work. What you don't want is to allow these default choices to define your life.

What if you used shadow comforts and time monsters as an early alert system, to show you if and how you might be defaulting on your desires? What if, sometimes, these choices could be messengers pointing you to a deeper need? Hiro Boga says of the relationship between craving and deep desire, "If you meet craving with curiosity and gratitude, rather than plunging headlong into suppressing its message by immediately satisfying the craving—which can never be satisfied, because it will keep pointing to the desire that underlies it— then it leads you deeper into communion with yourself, and with your world."

When I was lost deep in *why bother*, my shadow comforts and time monsters were book buying, lots of naps, answering email as soon as it came in, repeating the same kinds of work, worrying about my daughter and my mom, and eating lots of sweets. Hiro was right: none of that ever satisfied me. But what were my desires underneath, the desire that wanted to help me care again? Creating, being kind to myself, connecting, and taking in the sweetness of life. That's what I know now but not then. I would berate myself for being lazy and I'd make a strict plan to be more "disciplined" starting tomorrow. This never worked and it made it harder than ever to know what I wanted.

Compare that to what I chose for myself a few months ago. My mom was dying and I flew to Florida to be with her. Every day for the last week of my mom's life, I got up early and drove from my sister's house to memory care. On the

"The desire to be wholly alive suffices."

DANIEL ODIER, DESIRE

first day, I figured out where I could get food I liked along my route. I made a conscious decision to give myself all the noshing and crunching I wanted, but from food I enjoyed and that made me feel good. I used pleasure and comfort to make it more possible to stay awake to the wonder, sorrow, and intensity of being with my mom as she died. I wanted support to not miss or dodge anything—support to bother. I knew what I wanted, to be fully present, and I knew what would help me—food that comforted me, that I loved, but that didn't trigger my food allergies or numb me out. I also downloaded fantasy novels and read by Mom's side when I needed to escape but be close by and at night when I couldn't sleep. I supported my desire to be present to Mom's death not by asking myself to become a different person but by working with who I am. If I hadn't given thought to how shadow comforts would show up for me during this harrowing time, I would have numbed out and very possibly not been able to be present with my grief and my sister's grief. I wouldn't have been able to honor my deepest desire: to be present.

When we frame shadow comforts and time monsters as substitutions for true self-care or true desire, and we stop thinking about them as moral failures—which they never are— we create more space to make the choices we want and to shore our spirits up to bother more. We become curious, even grateful, that we have another chance to yet again live the life we want. This is so vital to understand: how you are presently comforting yourself is not wrong or bad; it's your best attempt at self-soothing and desire fulfillment. Self-blame and self-improvement will not help you experience more of what you want. Ever.

Carol was deep in the land of shadow comforts:

> It was the middle of the day, with so much work I wanted to do for my business, and instead I was eating my way through the pantry and watching shows on Hulu. There was a moment when I just stopped and realized the numbing had zero satisfaction. I wasn't getting anything out of it. It was like a switch on a set point for despair had flipped and I couldn't go back. I was craving something real, in a way that I crave kale after eating too much chocolate. I realized that what I thought was real, what I was chasing in my work, was not on point. I was

numbing out because all of my striving was toward a goal that I didn't want, and I avoided that truth by engaging in patterns that tried to quiet the noise.

I stopped, put away the chips, and turned off the computer. I hoped that what I really wanted would suddenly show up and I could dive into making that happen. But there was just silence. There was a feeling of something wanting to emerge but no clear action. Instead, I saw what I didn't want. I didn't want to numb out anymore. I didn't want to resign my hopes for a more satisfying life.

Those of us who struggle with addictions, eating disorders, and self-harm have a whole different level of fear around shadow comforts. Our brains react to craving in a way that means asking, "What do I really want?" is not always safe. Instead, we may need to ask, "What support do I need to stay sober and on my side?" Your primary need is to stay safe and then build a more intimate relationship to desire from there. Your focus is on being stable. There is all the time in the world to get curious about desire. You can and will still make room for desire and get your bother on, but first you must always take care of your sobriety.

I flirted with addiction in my twenties—cocaine, overeating, alcohol, men's attention. I was lucky

> It can be almost impossible to remember to replace your substitute desires with something more fulfilling, especially when you are stressed or exhausted or the outside world is cruel. Check out the extra help on offer at jenniferlouden.com/whybother.

that none of this killed me or even hurt me badly, especially because addiction runs in my family. My dad drank moderately but daily and told me he thought of himself as a controlled alcoholic. My mom became an alcoholic by my late twenties. I never knew how bad it was, since I lived across the country from my parents, but I saw enough ugly drunk episodes to know she had a problem. Dad would talk to her, I'd talk to her, she'd be sheepish and swear to cut back. And she would but she couldn't sustain it. I colluded with my parents by not intervening more. I told myself she couldn't change, what else did she have, she never drove drunk, it was my parents' lifestyle. I told myself there was only so much I could do. It still makes me sick to wonder what else I could have done.

In the last years of Mom's life, before she forgot to drink because of Alzheimer's, she got drunk most nights. We learned to pick her up for dinner earlier and earlier and give her watered-down wine with dinner. It was ugly and painful for all of us, although less and less for her as her memory gave way. I confronted her several times, as did Bob. I got her into therapy, but Mom told me after two sessions, "The therapist thinks I'm fine. I don't need to go back."

I still don't know why Mom drank so much, though I have my suspicions—she had a rough childhood, and she was sure her father was not her biological father but her mother would never tell her the truth. And I believe one reason she drank was her unrealized desires. She never was able or supported to become the subject of her own desire. She loved her daughters and my dad and making our lives beautiful, but that wasn't enough. After Dad died, she was briefly on her own and claimed her desires and enjoyed herself, even as she grieved Dad. She bought her first house by herself and lived alone for the first time in her life. She bought the car she wanted. She made friends, volunteered, even starred in a few local fashion shows. She fought to make a life for herself. And then Alzheimer's took that away, bit by bit.

My mom haunts me in a good way, reminding me to be brave enough to fight for my desires. Not to fight myself but to fight inertia, to fight the culture, to fight the ways I've internalized giving up on myself. To inquire daily, "How do I want to be the subject of my own desires?"

Having a healthy relationship with desire isn't about getting what you want, pooh-poohing what you want as impossible, or grasping after a craving. It's about staying with your desire and letting it teach you. To do that, you make room for discomfort, dissatisfaction, restlessness, frustration, and, yes, heartbreak. But the payoff is indescribable. There is a vitality and a truthfulness that comes from knowing what you want that connects you to your deepest values and helps you stand for what you truly care about. You *feel* why you bother.

The next time you reach for what could be a shadow comfort or time monster, pause. You can have whatever you're reaching for—promise yourself that—but why not be sure it's what you really, truly want and savor it fully?

Ask
yourself:
"Is this
what
I truly
want?"

———

Is this what I want? Or **Must this really be done right now?** If the answer is yes, then enjoy thoroughly or focus completely. If you aren't sure, have what you've already chosen while noticing if you are enjoying yourself. Are you grasping after something? Are you settling for a substitute? Are you displacing your desire by doing a chore or taking care of someone else first? Is that okay with you? Are you telling yourself there is no time for what you really want?

Is this what I truly want? If the answer is no, you might not know what you are hungry for. Very normal! Remember we don't live in a world that says, "Please take the time to get to know what you want and ask for it." You can experiment with various things to see if those feel more satisfying. You can settle and welcome what you are feeling and then ask again. If nothing comes, no worries. Give yourself the best you can and know that it's the asking that matters.

If there is something else I want more, even though I can't have it, can I let myself know what it is? You can't discover what you want or even might want if you immediately cut off your longings with a harsh "but I can't have it so there's no point in wanting it." You have no idea where your desire might lead you or what it might reveal to you. Breathe into the sensation of wanting, of longing, and of not knowing how or if your wanting will be fulfilled. Invite wonder in to be your companion. This moment of not knowing how or when or if is often exactly where your *why bother* is regenerated.

How Do You Want to Desire?

There is how you desire now, and there is how you want to desire. Writing that, I hear a voice in me pipe up, "You mean I get to choose?" Yes, you do. It is in the choosing that we keep the channel open to life and it is how we continually find the bright side of bothering.

You may need help learning how you want to want. We need role models who show us different styles of desiring, like Roxane Gay, Lindy West, Jonathan Van Ness, Maxine Waters, Ruth Bader Ginsburg, Maya Angelou, Elizabeth Warren, Emma Watson, Janet Mock, Desmond Napoles, Mary Oliver, Lizzo, Malala Yousafzai, Isabel Allende—people who live their desires openly and who talk about wanting in a positive light.

Women who love fashion find style icons for inspiration. Why not have a desire icon? One of my desire icons is my friend Chris Zydel. Trained as a therapist, she has taught intuitive painting for decades. She lives her desires brightly and boldly—in her jewelry, her marriage, her political views, her work, her love of color, her writing. She told me, "Around certain things (physical objects like jewelry, books, fun experiences, sex), I have a relatively unfettered relationship with desire. I know what I want, I want what I want, and I let myself *have* what I want. I *feel* the thing I want as an excitement in my body. And then I think about the thing I want, plan for it, daydream about it. I also have a hard time taking no for an answer around my desires. I will move heaven and earth to get what I want and rarely ever give up trying. Even when I am met with roadblocks and frustration and outright failure." She inspires me to be more exuberant in how I desire, and more playful.

Research desire icons for yourself. These are people who you imagine—in this case, projection is your friend—have a healthy relationship with desire, which is not the same as always getting what they want. You could interview a friend who seems like she knows something about desire or read about people who followed what they wanted or watch films or TV shows about people with a healthier relationship to desire. You aren't looking for perfection or even a happy ending—that's not always possible and not the point.

As you investigate, note if any fears or judgments come up about how these people lived out their desires. *Desire is not without cost.* You might become edgy or fearful about those costs. Talk your concerns out with a friend, therapist, or in your journal. There's gold in that rumbling of "Watch out! Go back! Bad idea!" Please don't shut down. Remind yourself it is safe to desire. You are *not* committing to anything or making a plan. You are opening to desire.

Desire Retreats

It's elegant, it's simple, and it's a wondrous way to reacquaint yourself with desire. All you do is set aside a clear period and do only what you want for as long as you want. I include this as part of all my retreats and it never fails to elicit big aha moments, even change lives. Karen told me at the end of a retreat that she'd been unhappy since her retirement sixteen years before and by asking "What do I want?" she rediscovered her *why bother*: "I'm going home so grateful and I can't wait to tell my husband how ready to be happy I am."

What it is about asking "What do I want?" that changes women? Well, we don't do it often, if ever. We go to work, we care for children or elderly parents, we exercise, we clean, we make meals: we do what we have to. Even our days off and our vacations can be about other people or getting stuff done—ticking boxes on the sights and the shows to see. A desire retreat is like being a child again on a free Saturday. It's deeply refreshing to do only what you want when you want, to pay attention and to heed what you want, instead of dismissing it out of hand. It's self-cherishing to drive to the market and get yourself a perfect mango just because you want it. It's self-regard in action, and it quickly teaches you so much.

For more pointers and support on doing your own desire retreat or to join a group desire retreat, jump over to jenniferlouden.com/whybother.

Let's break down the elements of a desire retreat.

1. Clear a period of time

You need a *clear period of time*, which means you know when you will start and end your retreat. It doesn't have to be a precise time, like ten a.m. It can be "I'll start when my partner leaves the apartment and end around four when I get ready to take my mom out to dinner." It can be the two hours you "find" when a client unexpectedly cancels or for the duration of your kid's swimming lesson or soccer game. The reason you need to know when to start is otherwise you might fritter your time away doing things you "need" to do or get sucked in by the internet. The reason you need to know when you will end is otherwise you might feel selfish or unmoored by giving yourself so much attention. I call this a clear period a container: life needs containment to come into form.

2. Do only what you want

The second element is to *do only what you want* for as long as you want. If you want to read a novel, read a novel until you notice yourself not wanting to anymore. Then ask yourself the gorgeous question, "What do I want?" and notice where that leads you. Maybe to the kitchen to eat a handful of chocolate almonds. But instead of shoving them in your mouth, you pay attention to how the almonds taste, how they feel crunching under your teeth, if you want another one. Then maybe you don't know what you want next, but instead of defaulting to doing laundry, prepping your kids' lunches, buying a birthday present for your best friend, or reading the news, you stay with asking "What do I want?" You might sit on the couch and put your hand on your heart and breathe through the panic of wanting to do everything all at once: sketch, read, practice yoga, go for a hike, look at those old scrapbooks, write a poem, drive to that town with all the murals and take pictures, and and and... or breathe through the panic of not knowing, of having no idea what you want. This is the whole point: to awaken desire.

3. It's not about what you do

When you haven't made time and space in a long while for the pleasure of asking yourself, "What do I want?" it can feel as if you've tapped a gushing well and you can't control it, or a dry well where nothing is coming up. Nothing to worry about—a desire retreat is less about having a wonderful experience (although that often happens) and more about listening to what attracts you. You keep breathing, pausing, asking, and telling yourself, "I can have more desire retreats." If everything you think about doing feels humdrum, check in. Are you putting undue pressure on yourself to have a spiritual and emotional awakening and to figure out everything about desire in one day? That will not happen and it doesn't need to. Perhaps what you need is rest. Your lack of desire might be a harsh inner voice insisting that rest is self-indulgent, you will never get up again, a good person never naps. Or maybe you are dismissing small inklings because they feel too odd or flimsy.

4. No appointments or musts

Desire retreats have a feeling of meditation because you stay present to what's appealing to you now. You don't want any appointments, not even fun ones, because you want to adjust what you do moment by moment. Know when the art museum is open or the drop-in painting class happens but don't commit to anything. Otherwise you aren't giving yourself a desire retreat, you're planning a fun day off.

I once decided during a desire retreat that I wanted to rearrange all my books in my office. Halfway through, the floor of my office covered in piles of books, I realized I didn't want to do that anymore. I wanted to go for a walk in the woods. For the next three weeks, I picked my way around those piles before I got the time to put them back on the shelves. I loved the mess and saw it as a sign of my desire heeded.

Start small, with an hour or two. With loving attention, greet any feelings of hunger for more time or restlessness or feeling that what you want is out of reach. Instead of pushing away whatever you are feeling or thinking, stay with it. The feelings, when met with curiosity and no agenda, will move and morph, and then you can go back to asking, "What do I want?"

Nothing is off limits. If you to watch seven episodes of *Buffy the Vampire Slayer*, finish your taxes, call a friend you had a fight with last week, shop for the perfect backpack, take a two-hour nap, don't judge. But do keep asking, "How does this feel? Do I still want this? Do I want something more? Different?" It is in the asking that you touch desire. That's what you're up to, that's the point. Fun, relaxation, and enjoyment are lovely by-products. The main attraction is making friends with desire.

Drop the Scenarios

Desire is present in every moment. It becomes more refined as we get more comfortable giving ourselves permission to know it and to choose ourselves in relationship to it. It gets less knowable when we project our desire into the unknowable future.

I was coaching a writer about to start an MFA in middle-grade fiction. She'd been a stay-at-home mom for the last thirteen years and she came to me for help to see herself as a writer. Five minutes into our conversation, she blurted out, "I'm afraid of success."

I sat up straighter, switched my teacup to my other hand. "Are you?"

She explained she'd had some success, and the feedback "had made me want to crawl under the kitchen table and barf," she said, even though the feedback was almost entirely positive. "I just know I'm going to publish novels that people will criticize and that makes me want to barf too, or I will become so successful that I will have to keep writing all the time and then my family will be neglected and the kids will hate me and..."

I smiled at her, never less than amazed at how clever our brains are at shutting down our desire. "I wonder if you're not afraid of success," I said, "but afraid of your vision of success?"

We get ahead of our skis, as the old saying goes, when it comes to desire. We jump into the future and map out all the ways what we want can go wrong—or right. We label those scenarios with all kinds of fancy psychological and spiritual terms that instantly become *the* truth we know will happen. Why bother to write a middle-grade historical novel if I will get slammed by the teachers' association or trapped by my success?

My daughter loved to sing as a child. A friend who was visiting from out of town heard her and said, "She has an amazing voice. She must take voice lessons. She must do something with her gift." I remember being repelled by her advice. If Lilly decided she wanted to pursue singing, I would support her any way I could. But to take a child's spontaneous, joyful expression and make it a thing that might get her something someday? It made me want to scream.

Treat yourself like I did Lilly when it comes to your desires. I believe we need to be supportive and appreciative of our desires, and that it's best to step away from commodifying what brings you to life. I know that might sound ironic from someone who sells her ideas. But I also know the cost of selling what is close to our hearts. It's easy to lose sight of what brings you alive and get trapped in your story of what you have to do or what people want.

Karen Rinaldi, author of *It's Great to Suck at Something*, makes the argument that we diminish ourselves and our lives because we refuse to suck at stuff: "Because we are so geared toward success and reward above all, we fail to set aside space in our lives to cultivate new talents and interests. That kind of cultivation will inevitably include fits and false starts. We'll almost certainly look foolish... When we approach something new, it seems like our first response is to try to dominate it. If we can't, we ignore it. By ignoring it, we solve one problem: we don't have to be inadequate at something, but we create another: we diminish our lives. We add another blank spot. Adulthood becomes a kind of accumulation of blank spots."

Reading that, I thought of my obsessive foray into art making about fourteen years ago. I'd make art instead of write—so much so that I almost missed a book deadline. I got paint and glue everywhere, on our oak floors, my clothes, even our antique Mission-style dining room table that I was so proud of. For the first year or two, it was the most creative fun I'd ever had. But then I began to wonder if I was any good and if I should do something with my art. That's when the joy went *poof!* I grew frustrated, started a million things and never finished anything, and eventually I quit. I didn't know how to suck, and I allowed the ever-present marketplace into my studio. Create for money, create things that were fantastic, or why bother? Why bother to create if you don't produce something that makes money or impresses people or garners you

"Appetite is . . . about the deeper wish . . . to partake of the world, to feel a sense of abundance and possibility about life, to experience pleasure."

CAROLINE KNAPP, APPETITES

millions of followers? This life-sucking story has stopped so many creatives and writers I've worked with and it is certainly one I've had to teach myself to keep thumbing my nose at. I've also witnessed an equally common story that your art or ideas should not be commercially successful or you've sold out. Better to be a poor but proud artist. What strikes me about both these stories is they stifle desire's expression. They muffle life with irrelevant narratives that make our worth all about the marketplace. I, for one, refuse to reduce my desires and my life force to a commodity, even if it is a commodity I am withholding.

A slightly different twist on desire and the marketplace is women who have been traditionally successful at one or more endeavors, but if they can't be sure they'll again experience the same level of success and achievement, they won't do anything, even something for fun, even something they want to do. Without outside affirmation, either in the form of money or praise, they stutter to a halt. They are also blinkering their desires.

For all of us, no matter our story, the most interesting thing about bothering again has nothing to do with what you excel at or what you can sell or refuse to sell, and everything to do with the way you live. The way you express the life force running through you. Step away from throttling desire by needing to do something with it, or refusing to do something with it, or needing to know how it will turn out. Let yourself simply enjoy yourself for now.

Relax Your Body

Desire likes a relaxed body. It likes wide, deep breaths that expand your ribs and plump out your belly. It likes a jaw that isn't super-glued with tension. It likes hands that are not gripping the steering wheel or pen like an eagle gripping her prey. It likes a rested body. It likes a tall spine, a half smile.

Desire is energy. It can't move freely if you're in a constant state of physical tension and immobility.

Immobility kills desire, as much as tension does. When *why bother* had me around the neck, I had to cajole myself to move. Not moving—not wiggling or dancing or walking or running or having sex—is a sign I'm afraid to feel my feelings or that I'm actively denying something I want to bother about. I used to restrict my movement as if I might get into trouble or unleash too much power. You wouldn't have known it to look at me—I'm a fidgeter par excellence—but I knew. I knew I was afraid of feeling too much life force, so I would grit and constrict and pretend I didn't want to be intimate with Bob. The energy of desire terrified me.

Even though I had several decades of serious yoga asana practice—which conceivably would have taught me to work with energy—it wasn't until I connected *relaxing* my body to *allowing* the energy of desire to flow that I began to venture back into life. Like a river: no forcing, no holding back. Rilke was onto something.

For a guided meditation to meet desire and additional resources to relax your body, go to jenniferlouden.com/whybother.

I still get stuck and constricted, and it always pushes me away from bothering toward self-doubt and shutting down. My go-to move is to tell myself, "Do anything." I can't say to myself, "Go to the yoga mat" when I'm stuck— it's too scary. Or even "Put on a song and dance" because again, too much. "Do anything" might be getting up from my office chair and walking out onto the deck to stretch or if I can't seem to make myself get up, stretching right there in my chair. I also drink a lot of water so I can use going to the bathroom as a chance to move my body and return to feeling life. *Do anything, move anything.* It makes a good mantra.

Speaking of mantras or little phrases to repeat when desire feels too much, too frightening, or forbidden, here are a handful I use and have given to students.

- There is more of life to come.

- It is safe to desire. I'm an adult and I can make it safe.

- I can experience more—more aliveness, more connection, more creativity—starting now. It's here *now*. I don't have to wait or ask for permission.

- I can rest in the gap between desire and satisfaction.

- Life is not a problem to be solved.

- I take responsibility for my desires.

- I no longer need to make myself small or hide from what I want in order to protect others.

- It is not about getting it right; it is about moving forward from what I feel and know now.

- I have permission to live my life for my purposes.

- This is life. I am so lucky to be here for this. For all of it. Even this.

Strain is unnecessary and unhelpful. Straining and tensing up sends a subtle message that you don't trust yourself or life to carry you forward. Relax and notice where and how the creative process of life is happening. If you tense up thinking about your "progress," you can see your worry as a sign you care about your future rather than a sign you aren't getting anywhere. Relax the body, move the body, remind yourself it's safe, and desire will flow into action.

Reflect

Can you allow yourself to be with desire without having to do anything with it? Can you celebrate desire's rising energy and let it vibrate and illuminate your being?

What is it like to position yourself as the subject of your own desire rather than the object of someone else's? In what situations is that easy, even automatic, and in what situations might it feel confusing or unsettling or selfish?

Do desire and greediness get tangled together in any area of your life? Do you judge yourself for wanting certain things?

When you look at how shadow comforts and time monsters show up in your life, what do you think you're truly desiring?

If you could have all that you desired, what would you be bothering about?

Taking action
is about opening
yourself to caring
and learning rather
than rushing to
certainty, success,
or pleasing others.

———————————

(9)

Become by Doing

Mind the Gap

When I work with writers full of self-doubt, I often say, "You become the person who can write the book by writing the book. You aren't that person yet and the only way to become that person is to write what you want to write." Or as Rollo May said in *The Meaning of Anxiety*, "One does not become fully human painlessly."

You've made space to learn what you desire; this stage— *become by doing* is about taking action on that desire. You take action on what's crooking its finger at you, twinkling here and there, mildly or madly of interest to you. It's not about what you do or what it gets you or how it adds up, but how you do it, how you open yourself to caring and learning anew. The point of the actions you take in this stage is about bothering rather than achieving, finishing, or arriving. Keep reminding yourself that while certainty and a positive outcome feel great, they truly are beside the point.

You rush to certainty when your emotional immune system is triggered. Most of us believe on some level that because we want something, we should be able to realize it without breaking much of a sweat. But there is always a gap between what you can do now and what you want to do. This gap is a beautiful, fascinating part of the creative process, a sign you're paying attention, tuning into desire. You're bothering again! If you weren't aware of the gap, what would ever change? Still, the gap is rarely an easy place to hang out, and so we deny it exists and get frustrated and quit or pretend we don't care about closing it and give up before we've started.

As you reengage with life, you try new things, which means you learn to make peace with the gap. *The gap will always be a part of a well-lived life.* It is never a problem, but you make it one when you see it as a sign of personal failure. Then you put your desires up on a high shelf, carefully wrapped in tissue paper in a protective box, where they can stay untarnished by life, forever unrealized, and you with them.

Instead, you could look at the gap as the place where creatives learn to be at home or at least learn to tolerate. Your brain and nervous system are not going to easily or automatically like the gap, not at all. But with practice, you truly can learn, no matter your wiring and personality, to be curious and even calm here. I told you the story of almost refusing Bob.

That was a gap I kept refusing to stand in, the gap of being committed to a man who wanted to be close, who wanted to spend time together, who wanted to know me. I kept trying to get away from him or fantasizing about a future in which I somehow knew how to be in this kind of close relationship.

What I finally learned to do, after I said yes to him in the hotel room, was to be right where I was—uncomfortable, not knowing what to do next, while asking myself, "What do you want to try here? Who do you want to be in this moment?" It was maddening and scary and painfully messy, but because I finally committed, because I forever closed the door to leaving, I stayed in the gap. And I would never have been able to have the life I've made if I didn't learn to do this.

Leigh is a multi-passionate creative who has a great story about spending time in the gap: "Three years ago, I came up with an idea for a board game. I tried partnering with various coworkers, but it was always a disaster. I did a workshop with a group to test the game. Also a disaster. I made other attempts, but the results were the same. I was humiliated and frustrated. I put the game on the back burner, which can be an incredibly important step in *why bother*. It gives you time to heal and forget the sharpness of disappointment.

"A year or two later, I tried again. I found someone through an online freelancing site who became my partner, and together we built a team who bothers about my idea. We just won a $200,000 grant from the Department of Education to build the board game that I started so very long ago. I bother

· because there is magic in creating something from despair, in standing in the gap long enough to keep trying."

One big difference between people who give in to the blank side of *why bother* and people who don't is their ability to stand in the frustration and uncertainty of the gap. Your brain loves certainty, but the creative process of life couldn't care less. It cares only about your becoming. Not arriving, not accomplishing, not finishing, not succeeᴅᴉ...ᴏ. ᴄcoming. *Living.*

Everything Is an Experiment

How do you live in the gap without forcing or pushing yourself or giving into fear and staying defended but cut off from life? How do you learn to be comfortable with the discomfort of not knowing and yet still experiment? It's simple. And sometimes, if you let it be, even easy.

You take your next inspired—or mildly interesting—action. *Mildly* is important. You need not wait around for bliss or clarity. Then you notice how what you did feels and where it naturally leads you next. This is the core work of this stage. It's so simple that you will second-guess it and try to complicate it. That's okay, we all do, and we can then head back to keeping it simple, sweetheart.

Because as you venture deeper into bothering again, the last thing you want to do is bury whatever is stirring in you under a big complicated plan. Plans are awesome, I love plans,

"Hope is definitely
not the same thing
as optimism. It is not
the conviction that
something will turn out
well, but the certainty
that something makes
sense, regardless
of how it turns out."

———————————

VÁCLAV HAVEL, DISTURBING THE PEACE

but they are for later. I love a story my nephew-by-marriage Randall told me during a visit. He had ended up in the emergency room with a panic attack, and after he found out he wasn't having a heart attack, he had to face the fact he was mightily sick of his job as a corporate recruiter: "I almost wish it had been my heart because that's easy to deal with. Change your diet, get more exercise. This was a much bigger reckoning." Randall and my niece had saved enough that they could afford for him to quit his job and explore *what's next* for a few months. Everything about Randall's approach and attitude made me grin. He's trying out ideas, not married to anything, not counting on his next career move to define his identity, and not rushing. "Everything is an experiment," he said.

Experimenting is what you need, along with plenty of self-compassionate grit to stay awake and wonder to keep you open-hearted as you do. Please:

Extend caring to yourself

Let's say you want to try rock climbing and you do not understand why that is part of your *why bother*, but it's showing up. But you're afraid of falling, of hurting yourself, of being too weak to pull yourself up the wall. Here comes self-compassionate grit to the rescue. "I care about my fear and I care about sticking with what's calling me. I can do both by finding a class that feels safe and taking my time learning."

Keep the promises you make to yourself

Self-trust is composed of making and keeping clear commitments, first to ourselves and then to others. Yes, you read that right. *First* to yourself and *then* to others. If you tell yourself that you will try a rock climbing class on Tuesday at five p.m. and then you don't, you are teaching yourself you can't trust yourself. You worry that you can't be trusted to care, to stay with the river, to bother.

But that doesn't mean to be hard on yourself when you break a promise to yourself. You're human. Life happens. But a woman who bothers is a woman who squarely and lovingly faces her broken promise with curiosity and honesty. "I said I'd go to class, and I didn't. I sat on the phone with that lonely, disgruntled client and let him bend my ear until it was too late to go. Huh, I wonder (there's wonder again) what was that about? What was I afraid of? Or what hadn't I truly greeted with self-compassion and attention?"

Or maybe you told yourself you would go to that five p.m. rock climbing class and then you realized it was impossible because you had too much on your plate. You made an unrealistic promise—and we will get to those in a moment—but for now, same deal: more self-compassionate grit. Compassion for yourself for thinking that you're superhuman and grit in looking at when you can reschedule. You might also call on desire and check in: "Do I still want to go to that class? Is rock climbing a genuine desire?"

Separate your mood from your desire

Responding to desire means you listen to how desire is calling you rather than asking, "Do I feel like it?" Our moods are influenced by what we are thinking, what we ate for lunch, how much stress we're experiencing, and a ton of unconscious processes (up to 95 percent of our brain function is not conscious). If we let our moods dictate our lives, we get lost in our stories and feelings, create more of the "same old, same old," or rely solely on effort and willpower to move forward, which is exhausting. Moods are as changeable as the weather and not a reliable criteria to base your life on.

Each time you do what you want, or don't do what you don't want to do, or you check in with yourself, you strengthen the understanding that you are not your mood, not your thoughts, not your stories, not how your brain keeps you safe. You have a choice, even if you are depressed and anxious, in pain, or overwhelmed.

Desire says, "Let's learn about racial injustice," or "Let's work in the garden," and your mood says, "When I feel like it." In that moment, lean on self-compassionate grit to move forward.

Try out one of these questions when you feel like not budging or like you must will your life to change:

- What could be my next simple step?
- Who could I ask for help?

- What would be enough for today?
- What do I need to stop and learn?
- Where am I hurrying and being unrealistic?

One of the best things I ever learned is that our thoughts are innocent. Your thoughts about how you are bothering or if something will work out or if you will be good enough are innocent. They need not mean anything or determine anything unless you want them to.

Most of all, becoming by doing feels good. Never putative, harsh, or like something you do to prove yourself. Self-compassionate grit helps you experiment by feeding your self-respect and self-trust. It's the backbone in *why bother*.

Your Signature Themes

I'm intrigued by the idea that we all have "signature themes"—particular ideas, interests, passions, or issues that keep returning to us, wanting to be explored and worked with. It's not what form these themes take that matters, but that they won't leave you alone, that they demand attention. They can be broad and universal—for example, standing up for children without a voice or nourishing people or making the world more beautiful—but they can also be more specific, like addressing racism in your profession or understanding string theory.

Why do these themes matter to bothering again? Because if you ignore or deny these themes before you fully explore them, you end up facedown in the gunkiest kind of *why bother*. They seem to hold a spark necessary to the creative process of living.

As you may remember, unbeknownst to me, my work had been motivated by my mom's lack of choices and agency. That was one of my signature themes hiding in plain sight, as they sometimes do: to help women own their desires and act on them. I ran from that for so many years and for so many silly reasons. That running was another big cause of me getting stuck again and again. I judged helping women as not hip enough—I wanted to be a cross between Tina Fey and Susan Sontag (at least now I have the gray stripe in my hair). Instead I felt like a cartoon character, especially when I gave a speech to a women's group and was presented with a scepter and crown to wear while I talked. Yes, I had named a character in a book and my company Comfort Queen, but I didn't want to be her.

When I did embrace my theme, I pressured myself to have all the answers and to change every woman's life at my talks and retreats. Then I would feel, naturally, frustrated and like a failure. I would tell myself I needed to do something different, but nothing ever stuck. Round and round I went.

But then I sold another self-help book and I couldn't write it. I spent several months trying to get words on the page, but I had nothing. I gave back the advance, and within six months

I moved my family away from our happy life in Santa Barbara to the Pacific Northwest where we could live more cheaply. I decided I would write fiction and coach women. But because I had panicked and not gone through the process you are going through right now, I never made the transition. I never let go of my business, my speaking, my website, or my retreats. I drafted a novel that showed real promise, but I never rewrote it—and every writer knows most books only work after diligent revision. My energy and dedication remained where they had always been: helping women make more of what they wanted. It kept pulling me back. Yet I didn't make peace with this pull until the last few years, after I wrote about my mom being blocked from working and I could see how that experience had shaped me. In telling that story, I finally found the energy and truth in my work.

This is not to say that writing fiction wasn't a true desire for me nor am I trying to make my past too neat of a narrative. Storytelling and a love of all things magical is another theme of mine, but I believe I didn't persevere in exploring that theme because I had shortchanged and belittled my other work.

Signature themes can become so obvious when you relax and get curious, and when you stop confusing them with your life's purpose. Your life's purpose is to live fully and beautifully as yourself. Signature themes give you pointers on how it might be fun to do that. Some stay with you your whole life, and some themes come along and shape a year or a decade or two. My friend Lisa went to the Wind River Reservation to write a magazine article about an Arapahoe horse whisperer and ended up spending much of the next decade with him and writing a wonderful memoir about the experience. This experience shaped her life profoundly and then it was time to let it go and move on to her next signature theme.

When I asked women in the weekly Oasis community about their themes, they shared:

- "fascination with depth, mystery, and devotion to creating beauty,"
- "facilitating excellence," and
- "celebrating resiliency and continuous growth."

More specific themes included:

- "finding and nurturing the holy and sacred in the ordinary and the everyday,"
- "I want to save relationships,"
- "gathering and sharing information with others," and
- "everything I do ends up having something to do with child abuse."

Your signature themes excite you, trouble you, animate you, make you want to take action. You can't *not* interact with them unless you do what I did and judge them as inferior or yourself as not up to the task, or you fill your life with so many other things that your themes have no room to speak up. Your signature themes beg you to become by doing something about them. It's not that you are servile to them, but that you look for the places where your themes and your desires and your energy and time overlap. I wish I could have relaxed and gotten curious about why I couldn't stop serving women and asked myself, "What is it I want to create, express, experience here?" and "What do women need that I want to give?" I flipped between thinking I had to serve women in a very particular way that I couldn't do and ignoring what was calling me entirely. The result was a ton of wasted time and frenetic energy.

I'm asking you to hold both. To look for the places where your themes and your desire overlap. To accept that some mysterious combo of personal history, culture, family, and maybe even destiny fashion your themes; it's up to you to work with them in ways you find fulfilling. Consider the idea that "each person enters the world on an essential errand that intends to make their life meaningful and purposeful," to quote scholar and storyteller Michael Meade in *Fate and Destiny*, and that our signature themes are part of this errand—hot little energy centers and fascinating clues that form your path. Meade says, "Being lost or confused is not the problem; not becoming what we love, that is a real problem. In learning what our souls love, we move near the divine, for love is a divine gift."

What if your signature themes are a love note from life itself? What if you don't have to wrestle them to the ground, make them into a lofty life purpose, or ever earn a dime from them? What if all you have to do is listen for them, open a window to them? What if all they want is for you to love them?

The single worst thing to do with this idea is to make it a big ding-dang-do. The second is to assume you have no signature themes. The third is to decide yours are beyond you, that's it too late or impossible or that you've been there, done that. But you won't do that because you already left behind those kinds of thoughts and beliefs, right?

Signature themes are rarely unique or highly specific. It's not about being special, it's about recognizing what's true for you. Forgo coming up with the perfect label; instead, look for the pulse of energy and urgency you feel when you let yourself own your themes.

Remember it's *not* about your business or figuring out how to make a living from your themes. Those things might well happen or not, but resist putting that weight on this exploration.

Treat this idea lightly. Consider these lines from the William Stafford poem "The Way It Is": "There's a thread you follow. It goes among / things that change. But it doesn't change."

Conditions of Enoughness

If your satisfaction, your self-worth, and your well-being depend on meeting someone else's standards or reside in a future in which you meet your goals, you will always feel not enough and you will always return to the blank side of *why bother*, no matter what you do.

That's partially because so little about modern life cel-ebrates having limits or using them to be more satisfied. Capitalism is based on unlimited growth. If you don't grow, you get punished in the stock market. Technology pushes us to transcend time, to be everywhere always. Some New Age teachings insist limits are negative thinking and everything is quantum connection, so if you are thinking correctly, you will have everything you want, at least in time. Even mindfulness can become a way to torment yourself to be increasingly more productive yet continuously chill.

The only thing is you're human and humans have lim-its. Limits to your time, limits to your energy, limits to your resources, and limits to how you are supported. Pretending you don't have limits or being pissed that you do is exhaust-ing, demeaning, and extremely demotivating. It interrupts what you're able to genuinely bother about next, filling your head with the earworm of "not good enough" and comparing yourself to others. Thinking you need to do more than you do takes you away from your true desires through exhaustion and should.

If you never declare what is enough for you around what you desire, you'll never be satisfied. If you don't know what is enough, you give desire no way to come into your everyday life. *You* get to declare what is enough—nobody else.

This is a subversive idea, and it is not—I repeat *not*—another goal-setting tool. To decide with clarity what is enough for you—for a day or project or exchange with another person or just about anything you can think of—enables you to:

- Move away from always pushing yourself to do more or prove yourself
- Build your self-trust as you make and keep clear commitments to yourself
- Create mini periods of settling, which help you do more of what you desire
- Cut down on procrastination because your brain will freak out less and be less uncomfortable when you've made your next step clear
- Celebrate what you do, instead of focusing on what you didn't do or thought you should have done
- Increase your agency and power because you stop allowing anyone else—your sister, your mother, your boss, the influencer on social media—to decide what is enough for you
- Connect desire with what is possible and with action

Enoughness—or what I call conditions of enoughness (COEs)—marries desire to possibility and action. Remember *you are the arbiter of enough*. Nobody else. Not even when you have standards to meet at work, deadlines, or other people critiquing your work. They get to have their opinion and you get to take that into consideration, so you can keep your job or get a raise or whatever, but only *after* you declare what is enough for you.

How do you make all this goodness happen? There are four elements to setting your COEs:

1. Name what is enough according to you, in facts.

That means they are free from opinion, assessment, and outcome. You can do this for anything—writing, a family dinner, a work report, exercise, decluttering, anything.

In naming what you will do in facts, you separate how well you do something from what you do. For example, when my mom was in the middle stage of Alzheimer's, I would use COEs for my visits. I might decide, "When my mother asks me to get the phone fixed, I'll repeat my version of the loving-kindness prayer silently. 'May I be at peace, may I be happy, may my heart remain open, may I be present to this moment.'" The phone worked fine, only she had forgotten how to use it. If I had said to myself, "I will not get annoyed with my mom when she asks about the phone for the sixth time today," I'd be relying on something out of my control. Focusing on something I could do helped me be more patient.

"I will write 500 words before checking email" is something you can do. "I will write 500 brilliant words before email" is not because what are brilliant words? According to whom? You, in a good mood? Your partner, when she reads your pages? Right there is where we lose our way. We have to decide for ourselves, again and again, what is enough.

When you place your well-being and even your self-worth on outcomes you can't control, unsurprisingly, you lose your center and your self-leadership. From there, it's easy to slide into *why bother*. Because if you can't find a loving partner or get pregnant or ace the GREs or sell your novel for a big advance, really, why bother? This is how most of us approach what we want: we choose an outcome and then we paddle as hard as we can to get to it. Which is fine, so long as we remember the outcome is not who we truly are or where our satisfaction lives.

When you decide what is enough for you, you may still want a particular outcome, which is normal: you're human. Here's an example: I want you to love this book and give it to all your friends and have your book club read it. But if I focused on that while writing, oh what a hot mess I'd have been. Nothing I wrote would have been good enough. You still want what you want, but you learn to keep putting your energy and power in the only place it matters: on what you can do.

2. Decide for how long, how often, or some other measurement.

Once a week, for an hour, before bed for a month, my target heart rate, during my commute, Fridays from Memorial Day to Labor Day.

A measurement is the clearest way to know when to stop and say, "That was enough."

For example, you plan to strength train for twenty minutes, three times between now and Sunday. To spend one hour calling donors for the women's shelter auction. To name three things you're grateful for when you brush your teeth every night for a week. To call your dad on Saturday about an hour before you leave for the concert.

This part might sound strict or confining and it's not meant to be; it's instead meant to give you a measurement to rest in. "I need to call donors" can quickly feel daunting and become something you procrastinate about, then do, but then decide the other volunteers did a better job. Or calling donors turns into a time monster and eats up all your settling down or creative time because it's comforting to do something concrete and not comforting to hang out wondering what you want to bother about next. When you give yourself a measurement, you're saying, "This much is enough. Why? Because I say so."

3. Be sure what you are declaring is possible for you, given you're a human and not a robot.

Are you asking too much of yourself given your energy level, your to-do list, your previously scheduled commitments? Are you thinking today is the day when everything goes perfectly with nary a traffic jam, no last-minute emergencies with kids or elderly parents, no spilling coffee on your blouse, oh and you can work twelve hours without a break and faster than you ever have? Declaring what is enough means you remember your human-scaled life and that crap *always* happens and that bathroom breaks and sitting down to eat lunch does not make you a lazy putz.

4. When you finish what you said you would do, acknowledge yourself.

Celebrate in some small way. Give yourself a thumbs-up. Say to yourself, "Good job, I'm proud of me. Damn I'm good! Did it! Good job, Sunshine! Whoosh! Score!" Stretch, dance, shimmy, smile.

Keep your focus *not* on how you *did* but on celebrating that you did what you did. What *you* declared is enough.

You might be tempted to skip celebrating because it's not something most of us feel comfortable with—too close to bragging and calling attention to yourself and inviting disaster, because who knows if you can do it next time? If you're accustomed to celebrating only if you think you did a good job according to someone else's standards, that's the habit you're breaking. Take back your power and your joy!

If you can't think of how to celebrate, watch a replay of your favorite sports person winning or find a video of kids celebrating something. Celebrating is natural: it's just been shamed out of us. Growing up, I often heard, "Don't get a big head." My emotional immune system still gets triggered when I stretch myself as I have in writing this book. "You don't have what it takes. You're getting too big for your britches," opines my inner itty-bitty-shitty committee. Celebrating helps train our brains to notice that it feels good to do what you said you would and that you can trust yourself to keep your promises. Having a sense of autonomy and personal competence is profoundly motivating and gives you tangible proof when your inner critics pipe up.

Which means please celebrate even when your inner mean selves are catcalling you and demanding you do more, more, *more*. Marcy used COEs for gardening: "After I cleared the understory from one big bush, I sat on the porch and enjoyed my garden for a few minutes. In the past, I would have pushed myself to clear another bush and then another until I was exhausted and my back hurt because that's what good people do. I sat on the porch congratulating myself each time I finished a bush and it changed everything."

> Download a template and an audio guide on more ways to use COEs at jenniferlouden.com/whybother.

Joy shared that "COEs are permission to say, 'Yes! Good, I did enough.' Rather than beat myself up because I didn't do more," while Kendalle finds them "a way to settle into the core of your life."

Email, social media, smartphones, and work that has no boundaries—along with the collective mood of endless self-improvement, life hacks, and Instagram-filtered "authenticity"—eat at us. If we aren't building a multi-billion-dollar company, learning Italian, doing our Kegels, composing an opus, meditating twice a day with a top-secret mantra, making vegan meals full of micronutrients from sustainable local ingredients, keeping in touch with our 700 friends, visiting our parents, helping our kids get ahead, stopping the climate crisis while wearing a chic ethically made outfit, then how could we ever dare say we are enough? And if you can't do all that, then why bother doing much of anything?

Every week in the Oasis, my online community, we wrestle with what we want and what we can actually do that week, given our human-scaled life and our ongoing commitments. *Deciding is hard work.* But when we refuse to choose, we abdicate our lives. I spend an hour or more every week choosing what I will do and when. It takes that long both because the choosing is hard but also because it means breaking down what I am doing into small clear steps. I don't use COEs for everything on my list—lots of things don't need that kind of boundary—but using COEs for things like writing, running, and starting scary projects has taught me to always break things down so you know where to start and when you are finished. This is one of the best ways to prevent your emotional immune system from freaking out. When you read a list that is filled with vague tasks and too many of them, you often choose to procrastinate because it's too overwhelming. Before my last *why bother* time, I believed I could do everything and more in one day, a superhuman without a cape. It seems like a tiny thing, but learning to jot down small steps that were crystal clear—and only as many of those small steps as I could actually, honestly do that day—was one of the daily choices that freed me to get on with my life.

COEs takes ongoing discernment and adjustment. Holly wrote me about how she got off track: "When I first started using COEs, they were absolutely amazing but then they weren't. I quickly stopped meeting them and I felt awful. It wasn't until I recognized that my average—what was dependent only on me on an *average* day—was way too high. I had to work to get to what average really is. I still have trouble and find myself pushing the bar higher and higher, but now I know to recognize what I'm doing and drop back down. I can adjust without feeling like I'm failing."

Kendalle discovered something similar: "I forgot conditions of enoughness protect me from overdoing. Last night, I was supposed to stop working on my in-basket at 8:15 p.m., but I was feeling good, I wasn't tired, and so I kept going. Today, I felt it. It was too much. I pushed myself and then I crashed." This is a wonderful opportunity to adjust your COEs downward; it's not a sign they aren't working.

My friend, author, lawyer, and activist Marianne Elliott has used COEs for years: "Sometimes I forget how well this works for me and I drift back into traditional to-do lists, which are not time-bound or realistic and which never let me feel satisfied. I start to feel edgy all the time and, yes, unsatisfied, and I remember eventually and come back to the satisfaction approach."

If you try COEs and it feels crappy or overly complicated, run yourself through these trouble-shooting questions:

- **Am I using facts or assessments to declare what will satisfy me?** Facts are your friend.

- **Am I squeezing in more because it's been going so well?** That's called raising the bar and it will make you feel the opposite of satisfied.

- **Am I trying to apply COEs to every area of my life and feeling overly rigid?** Try using COEs sparingly, especially at first. Otherwise it can feel overwhelming and be too much work.

- **Am I rebelling against declaring a time element or other measurable quantity?** Don't like being human? It's fun to get all "unlimited potential" and "positive affirmation" on yourself, until it isn't. Human life has limits: that's what makes it precious and worth fighting for.

- **Am I skipping celebrating what I did and taking a breath or two to rest there?** Sweetie, give yourself some credit.

- **Are my COEs infused with desire and choice?** We all have to do stuff we don't want to do, and COEs can help break down the crap so it's not so onerous. But keep a lookout for making COEs a stick you beat yourself with versus a way to bring desire into form and yourself back into your life. This tool is meant to put you in the middle of your life, to give you a concrete and simple way to keep becoming. Make sure you are using it that way, at least some of the time.

Is Compromising Allowed?

Is it okay to coast, to phone it in, to stay where you're comfortable but not challenged; to remain in a relationship that's less than what you want but offers comfort, stability, and continuity; to stay in place where you have history but not love? As long as you honestly face and *choose* the compromise you're making, shoulds have no place in your realignment.

Brianna stayed in her less-than-fulfilling corporate job because it paid well and she wanted to fund her daughter's college tuition, but she didn't use that an excuse to give up on life. She found her *why bother* in mentoring new employees, starting an inter-office campaign to address implicit bias in hiring, becoming a competitive cyclist, and learning to sail. *Why bother* doesn't have to be about your career.

Or your love life. After Oliver's partner died, he said, "Our kids and my friends pressured me to date and at first I agreed, but then I realized what I wanted. Not love, not another intimate relationship, not even sex, but friends, women and men, I could share the world with. My kids told me I was giving up, but I knew what felt right."

For Maurine, it was about not pushing herself again: "I had a very successful business that I sold at a fairly young age. For years afterward, the pressure was to do it again, and bigger. I even had a coach tell me I was playing small."

For Dakota, it was not attending graduate school: "All my college friends are already earning a ton of money or are in grad or medical school. I pushed myself to apply and was accepted to an international development PhD program. Then I started having horrible nightmares and developed a painful skin rash. It was so hard to admit to myself that I don't know what I want, but I do know I don't want to go to graduate school."

Whatever you choose is perfect when it's your examined choice framed within your real needs and responsibilities. What you want to stay away from, besides doing whatever everybody else wants, is waffling. If you repeatedly say to your family and friends, "I'm going to _____"—whether that's get a new job, train for a 5K, submit your poetry, start dating, move to a new town, or adopt a kitten—and *you never do*, you're anchoring yourself on the icky side of *why bother*. What you're doing, besides annoying the crap out of your friends and family, is creating a chronic expectation of failure. You're teaching yourself you can't be trusted to honor what you want.

Waffling once hollowed me from the inside out. It's exhausting to second-guess yourself all the time. Instead of getting quiet and asking myself what I wanted and what my life needed, I went on a draining and expensive search for someone else to tell me what to bother about: experts, coaches, business consultants, even people I was envious of. I stopped trusting myself to listen for and then commit to my desires.

Everything changed when I said yes to marrying Bob. That was the most frightening commitment I could make, and a decision I could never half-ass my commitment to because this precious man's heart was at stake. If I said yes, I had to mean it. After that, I found it was possible to go all in on my work and my health—which didn't mean I suddenly had a ton of success or felt like a million bucks. There were wins and improvements and setbacks. The difference was that I was completely committed to owning what I wanted and declaring what was enough for me. And doing that made it easier to handle the setbacks.

I would never have copped to being somebody who hedged her bets or waffled. I saw myself as a very decisive woman. It's almost impossible to see where our emotional immune system is protecting us, so it can be worthwhile to note how often you aren't all in or to ask kind friends and family, "Do you see me equivocating about what I want? Very often? Does my butt have divot marks from living on the fence?"

You may well decide, "Nope, I will not go back to school," or "I'm not getting a divorce," or "I'm not coming out to my mom," or "I'm not opening my own business." Going all in can mean walking away from desires you aren't turned on by enough to uproot your life. Commitment can look like saying, "Not the right time," or that your family or community matter more. Saying no can be even more freeing than saying yes: you are firmly declaring what you won't bother about. You may need some time to adjust or grieve, but know the energy you've been spending going back and forth, starting and stopping, asking me or them, can now be freed for what you really want. Don't worry if you don't know! How could you when you've been consumed with waffling? Flip back to the Settle chapter, and go ahead and settle down. Remember, there is a natural creative process at work. It's been waiting for you to say yes to it. Thankfully, now you have.

What might be your personal tipping point? Is there a decision, choice, or commitment that could set you free? It could be in your work life or creative life or relationship or health. It might be a yes or a no, but it must have that same irrevocable *this is it* energy behind it.

Bothering Needs Embodiment

I took up running and, a year later, when I was a month shy of my fifty-fourth birthday, trail running. I promised myself that when I moved to Colorado, as part of my going all in on life, that I would say yes to every invitation, every adventure, even if I was scared or didn't feel great. I joined the neighborhood book group. I signed up for a writing class a friend had recommended because she thought the teacher and I would become friends, and we did! I went on pub crawls with my new neighbors, despite telling myself I was too socially awkward. I was so surprised I wasn't exhausted by this level of connection and getting to know people. Usually I would be. I believe it's because I was in touch with my desire to build a new life, so I was willing to stretch myself, and because I was willing to leave behind my stories that I don't belong (more on that later).

I learned about a running/walking group coached by one of my neighbors, Jabe. I made myself go, even though I was nervous about not knowing anybody. I planned to walk because running was not something I would ever do. I'd had two knee surgeries in my twenties and early thirties, and I could not, would not, run.

But there was only one other walker that evening, Kelli, and while I immediately liked her, she walked slower than me. I needed to get in my exercise for the day, my driven self said, but it would be rude to walk off and leave her so I said, "I think I'll try this running thing" and off I trotted. "Wow," I thought, "I am running." Then, between gasps for air, because after all I was 5,000 feet above sea level and not a runner, I thought, "This is fun." I ran all of 150 yards before I had to walk. I kept that up, running and walking, until I could see the rest of the crew running back toward me and I turned around so I could meet them at the car.

Four and a half months later, I ran my first half marathon in two hours and twenty minutes.

I promise I will not be that annoying person who tries to convince you to become a runner. This is about being embodied, not about being a runner. I found running super-charged my strength and faith in myself. This may have as much to do with the benefits of intense aerobic activity on my mood as anything else, but still it was so remarkable, I thought it worth

"The Church says:
The body is a sin.
Science says:
The body is a machine.
Advertising says:
The body is a business.
The Body says:
I am a fiesta."

EDUARDO GALEANO, WALKING WORDS

picking apart to see what might be useful for you as you think
about embodiment and bothering.

Running taught me how to not give in to discouragement.
As I've said, for years I unconsciously hid from what I wanted
behind a low-grade hiss of pessimism. You can't doubt yourself when you're running because when you do, it saps your
energy like someone swapped your legs for concrete pillars.
You can feel the effect of your self-doubt or self-judgment
immediately. You might say to yourself, "I'll only run to the
end of the fence and then I get to walk," and that's very different from saying, "I will run to the end of the fence and then
quit because I'm too slow and I'll never ever be able to do this
and I suck." It's a powerful immediate feedback loop.

Running showed me I could do something difficult and
be comfortable in the discomfort of doing it. Before, when
I didn't know how to bear the discomfort, I'd either pushed
myself or given up. The first time I ran twelve miles, I burst
into tears. I'd made it through something I was sure was
impossible. Every time I kept my commitment to train a certain number of miles in a week, do speed work or hill repeats,
or simply put on my running shoes and got out the door to
the closest trail, a flat stretch of dirt with a beautiful view of
the Flatirons in one direction and Longs Peak in the other, I
gave desire a stronger form, a musculature, to run through.
Embodiment links commitment.

Another thing running taught me is the power of support.
I hadn't had many mentors or teachers in my life who helped

me grow. Jabe is one of the best. Stretching after that first run, Jabe looked at me closely and then said, "You are a natural runner."

I said, "But I don't run."

She shrugged. "You're just getting started."

I was?

Jabe saw me. It's her talent, seeing people and giving them the support they need. Being seen by her changed how I saw myself, helped me to write a new story that included the identity of "runner." It made my newly found commitment more robust; you could say it gave it lungs and legs. Jabe saw something in me that I didn't see in myself, didn't even consider a remote possibility, which made me ask myself, "What else might I be capable of?" This can be so helpful when you are trying out new desires. Sometimes we need someone else to say, "Why not?" or "Of course!" to get us—or keep us—in the flow of life.

Of course, you don't need challenging physical activities to bother. I know how lucky I am to be able to run or even to walk down to the corner restaurant. You may live with a chronic illness, a physical disability, worn-out knees or hips. You may have sworn off exercise years ago because of an exercise disorder. You may simply hate to sweat. I'm not pitching you on spandex and half marathons. I'm pitching embodiment. *Bothering needs embodiment.*

Another way to think about it is that your body is the fastest way in, the fastest way to decide what to not bother about

"I don't think that loving yourself is a choice. I think that it's a decision that has to be made for survival; it was in my case. Loving myself was the result of answering two things: do you want to live? 'Cause this is who you're gonna be for the rest of your life. Or are you gonna just have a life of emptiness, self-hatred, and self-loathing? And I chose to live, so I had to accept myself."

LIZZO

and what to bother about, the fastest way to support your real desires, the fastest way to stop waffling, the fastest way to feel your way into lasting change.

The body knows. Your body wants to explore feeling safe in its own skin again. It wants to breathe more fully and deeply so your nervous system isn't on high alert all the time, sapping your energy and messing with hormones and adrenal glands. The body wants to experience joy, to rejoice in being here, in being alive. It has so much to say about the choices that face you, so much to remind you of and point out, through its shivers and how it recoils and how it yearns to touch that soft green wool or plunge its hands through mud or dance and sway.

Oh, our poor bodies. Punished by us and others and the world we live in. Made to sit in chairs and under fluorescent lights, having to show up according to a schedule rather than their circadian rhythms, being fed food that makes them feel like poo, being judged at every turn for not being thinner or white or straight or able-bodied. Our bodies are where trauma and shame and rejection are imprinted. Our bodies need so much time and attention, and they are always asking for more. More naps, more mangos, more touching, more love.

It sure seems easier to forget about them, to be a giant head on a stick, free of having to accept, love, talk to, be in relationship with all this flesh.

Somedays I wish it worked. But it doesn't. Running taught me that too. Running taught me that I can't bother if I don't come down into my body. Not for the long haul. If I spend all my time in my head, I float away from what's real and what I want. I believe my stories and forget to check in with how things feel. I believe my mind telling me I can only speak up or take action if I know exactly what to say or exactly what I want—instead of my body's knowing, which is simply, "Something is not right. Something is off."

What's your body telling you about what it needs? And about what it wants to bother about? Nothing to figure out or fix, only a friendship to deepen, a home to love. Get help if it's too scary to come into your body alone. There is good help out there and it's worth the effort to find it. One moment your body may want a gentle walk or a bath or to find a therapist who is trained in a form of somatic therapy. Is it chair yoga? Screaming at the top of your lungs? Climbing a mountain, learning to swim, asking yourself every hour, "What does my body need now?" Buying a stand-up desk or a better office chair? Having a meeting while walking outdoors? Is it giving up smoking, drinking, dieting? Is it eating exactly what you want when you're hungry? Is it listening when your gut says, "This situation isn't good for you," and acting on this knowledge?

Come on over to jenniferlouden.com/whybother for an embodiment playlist.

How does your body want to accompany you and lead you into your renewed life? Invite all of yourself to the party, or the party will only be half as much fun.

Choosing Is Your Art

"But there are so many things I want to bother about," some women say to me. "I can't choose, or at least not for long, and then I go back to being stuck." Choosing to go deeper or make a declaration of what you want to do can cause inner rebellion and confusion. Do you even have to choose? What about being multi-passionate? Wanting to bother about a bunch of interesting things is wonderful and you are a human, which means you live in time and three-dimensional space. You cannot exist in seven places at once except in your imagination, which is cool but not the only place you want to live.

Choosing is desire in action. Choosing is declaring, "I care about what I care about enough to settle and focus *for now*." Those last words can be a great comfort to any part of you that feels choosing is akin to being buried alive. *For now.* Nothing is forever. There will be time for many more choices, micro and macro. But if you don't choose now, many of your future choices can't happen. Choosing now paradoxically means you can choose even more later!

Choosing is not death to your various imagined futures and ideas, to the parts of your personality that are afraid they will never get to come out and play. If choosing makes it hard to breathe, start a notebook and write down every desire you have. I keep a lovely notebook for this, a fancy one I got as a gift and then never used because it felt too fancy for my scrawled thoughts. I write slowly and neatly. I do this to honor all these ideas, and after I write, I say to myself, "I love you. And for now, I'm doing _____. But you are in the book and not forgotten."

You might also ask yourself: "Who am I rebelling against?" I've found a lot of my clients and students are rebelling against someone else defining what being finished means. But you're in charge of that now, not a teacher or parent or boss or the swim coach who screamed at you until you finished what he said you had to finish. You get to decide what finished means. You get to decide what enough is. Fear of choosing may mean you're ceding your power to someone else and their definition of finished, whether that's a long-gone parent or the shadowy "they" we all reference. Counter this with conditions of enoughness: take the time to choose enough and see if choosing what you want to focus on grows more easily.

Another choosing conundrum has to do with business and can be especially sticky for solopreneurs who may feel that anything they choose has to fit within their personal "brand." I will refrain from ranting too much about this, except to say your soul is not toothpaste. It is never for sale. Everything you're curious about and want to explore does *not* have to be packaged, Instagrammed, and monetized. Social media has amplified the idea that "our basic humanity is... an exploitable viral asset... that selfhood exists in the shape of [a] well-performing public avatar," to quote from Jia Tolentino's first essay in *Trick Mirror*. Forcing yourself to think this way can somersault you right back to blahville, because what you want can start to feel as if it's a way to get more likes instead of a way to get back into life—very different things! It can make your caring feel shallow, performative, and false even when it isn't. Throw sharing out the door. *For now.*

Jeffrey had exactly that experience as he was exploring what he desired: "I thought it might be traveling around South America in a van, having adventures, and that I could make money by companies paying me to highlight their products. I'm a good photographer and surfer and rock climber and I knew people who were making it work, so it wasn't an insane idea. But within a month, I hated it. I felt as empty as I had back in New York making ads. I just hadn't given myself enough time and space to find what mattered to me."

You become the person who trusts the natural creative flow of life by *choosing*. Choosing love, choosing with enoughness, choosing knowing full well that everything changes, which means you will always be choosing. Choosing is jumping in the river of life every morning with a big grin and a *Cowabunga!* or sitting by the shore, sipping a cup of excellent fair-trade coffee until you wake up enough to slip in the current, sighing, "This is my life, I don't get a redo, so let's see what today will bring."

Learning to Choose Me

Desire without agency can look like you're bothering, but as I know only too well, it might look good but doesn't feel satisfying. Case in point: my obsession with getting on *Oprah*. It was 1998, smack in the middle of the era of Oprah turning authors into household names. My fourth book, *The Woman's Retreat Book*, had recently been published. Visualizing what you want had become a mainstream idea. I wanted a big bestseller again. So I copied the bestseller list from *Publishers Weekly* magazine, whited out the number one non-fiction title, and carefully inked in my book title. I glued that to a piece of slippery white poster board, followed by a photo of Oprah and me, arranged to look like we knew each other and were about to clasp hands. I cut out words from magazines, like a kidnapper turned conjurer, spelling out what Oprah would say about the book: "Changed my life. Everybody should read this!" I propped the poster board on the mantel of our fireplace, added a copy of my book, a crystal someone had given me, a statue of Ganesh (the Hindu elephant god who removes obstacles), and a picture of Chris and Lilly.

I walked by the fireplace many times a day. I'd glance at my Oprah altar, and my jaw and hands would clench, my eyes tighten. I willed my desire to happen. One day Lilly found me there, glaring at the poster board.

"Momma, I want to see." She tugged at my pant leg and I lifted her up, my face flushing. I'd assumed my wishful display was far enough above her head, literally, or that my lunacy was invisible, like when Lilly was a baby and thought if she hid behind her hands we couldn't see her.

She studied the arrangement. I inhaled her dense, doughy smell and tried to snuggle my head in her neck, but she pulled away. "Momma," she said, and pointed at Oprah, "do you like her?"

"I don't know her but..." I trailed off. Lilly fixed her blue eyes on me. Even at four, she had a penetrating stare that made me feel busted unless I told the absolute truth. I shrugged, put her down. "I'd like her to like me," I mumbled but she had already run to her Polly Pocket toys strewn across the living room rug as if a miniature tornado had struck a tiny town.

I picked up the painting I kept nearby and covered my wishful display, tucking the poster board behind it, and went into the kitchen to start dinner. It embarrassed me that my little girl had caught me in my childish games. But still I kept the vision board there, sneaking peeks when nobody was around. I wanted this so intensely.

A few weeks later, on a hot summer morning, I went in search of Chris to discuss our childcare schedule. It was so hot, all I had on was shorts and a jog bra. We were making plans when the phone rang.

Chris handed the receiver to me with an odd look. "Honey," he whispered, "she says she's a producer from *Oprah*."

I wiped my palm on my shorts. I wished I was wearing something crisp and tailored, that my toenails were painted, that I didn't smell musty. My hand was sweaty on the receiver.

"This is Jennifer." I almost asked if it was my friend Barb, trying to fool me.

The producer didn't waste a moment. They had a segment idea for "women afraid to eat alone in restaurants" and I'd be a great expert to have on. My first thought was "Why don't they just take a book with them?" and my second was "She isn't saying what I want her to say. That Oprah loves my book. Loves me."

What I said out loud is "I can't believe this is really happening."

I heard her but I didn't really hear her when she cautioned me: "You will only be a guest expert. This isn't a segment about your book." She couldn't have been clearer, but all I took in was "I'm going to be on *Oprah*." As I agreed to fly to Chicago in just over a week to counsel women on national TV who were afraid to eat alone in restaurants, I felt, oh so faintly, a drumbeat of warning.

I hung up, grabbed Chris in a big sweaty hug. "I'm going to be on *Oprah*! I'm going to be on *Oprah*!" As he swung me around, a gap between what was happening and what I wanted to have happened opened. I ran right in. Even as we went upstairs to get something cool to drink and call my parents, I forgot why I would be on the show.

I stood in the green room wearing my friend Susan's blue suit with a pleated short skirt, stockings, and blue suede heels I'd bought two days before in a panicked shopping trip. I hated suits, stockings, and heels. I was impersonating someone in this outfit. "Why aren't I someone who has clothes she likes in her closet?" I berated myself as I paced around the green room, passing the food spread again and again, craving a bagel but not allowing myself. I'd ruin my lipstick and get food in my teeth.

There was a commotion out in the hall. I looked up and there was Oprah, walking down the hall. She was dressed in a casual green cardigan and white pants, a happy garden-party outfit. The exact opposite of my banker-cheerleader suit. Her arm was slung around another woman and she was laughing. She glanced at me as she passed the open doorway, raised her hand briefly from the woman's shoulder. The heavy white stage door clanged shut behind her. I was alone again.

At that moment, it occurred to me that the day might not go the way I'd intricately fantasized for so long. That what I believed was waiting for me on the other side of being on *Oprah*—becoming a famous author with millions of copies of her book in print and Oprah's stamp of approval—wasn't there. This day was in fact no big deal.

I'd had intimations of this already. The invitation to coach women afraid to eat alone was the first, but then, on the plane, I sat next to a woman who asked me why I was flying to Chicago. I enjoyed the moment, anticipating how impressed she would be, even spinning a quick scenario of her asking for my autograph. "I'm going to be a guest on *Oprah*," I said.

She laughed and lightly punched my shoulder. "Me too!" She leaned closer. "But I can't tell you what's going to happen.

It's a secret." I stared at her. "But this is *my* big moment," I thought, the one I had visualized a million times, built an altar to, asked my readers to write to Oprah about, visualized with my jaw clenched. Now this woman was telling me she was not only on the show but part of a secret? I grimaced, murmured something about how great it was for her, pretended to go back to reading my book.

The monitor in the green room came on, filled with the show's logo, and then the set. I watched the first guest, a photographer, mumble his way through his interview. Slumped in his chair, he was almost inarticulate. Something about him not caring enough to sit up straight and speak up made me feel even more addled. Did he not know what a big deal this was?

His segment mercifully, finally, ended. I checked my lipstick in the mirror over the bagels, messed with my bangs. I looked pale. I pinched my cheeks. This was it! I walked to the open doorway, waiting for my producer to appear. No one came. The commercial for Tide ended and Oprah reappeared on the monitor. "You all know my very favorite author is the magnificent Toni Morrison and that my favorite book of hers is *Beloved*." I started sweating. I was supposed to be on by now. Oprah enthused more about *Beloved* and then the woman from the airplane stood up in the audience and mock-yelled at Oprah that *Their Eyes Were Watching God* was a much better book and Zora Neale Hurston was a much better writer. The young woman didn't give in when Oprah pushed back. The back and forth went on and on. "She was just an audience plant, not a real guest like me," I told myself. This is no big deal.

My producer bustled in. "It's time." "Wait," I wanted to say. "I have to pee, I want to change clothes, I want better hair, I want this to go differently." I nodded and followed her into the studio. "We've had to cut your segment from eighteen minutes to eleven. The piece about which writer is better went long."

"Oh" is all my tiny mind squeezed out.

The studio was freezing. The audience stared at me blankly. Oprah glanced at me from the edge of the stage where she sat, then went back to reading her notes.

I sank into the chair above her, understanding why the photographer looked like a broody child—it was a very deep chair and awkward to be on stage all alone, looking down on Oprah. I tried to perch on the edge. I noticed my shoes and remembered that when I had balked at the cost, Susan said, "Oprah loves good design. She will respect you for having those shoes." But as far as I could tell, Oprah did not notice my shoes. Or me.

Suddenly, we're on. The audience looked at me. My friend Barb, who happened to be in Chicago for a meeting, was sitting in the back row of the metal bleachers. She waved and I was briefly tethered to reality. Oprah addressed the camera. "My guest is a fan of 'parties for one.'" She said something about loving to start her day with a candlelit bath. She looked up at me. "Why are parties for one so important?"

"When you undervalue what you do, the world will undervalue who you are."

OPRAH WINFREY

Weeks later, when the episode aired, I sat in my living room with almost everyone who has been important to me in the last eighteen years. They crowded around our small TV, watching my reaction. When I saw myself on the screen, I was startled. My hair was styled unflatteringly, bangs parted in the middle, and I looked like I was about to bolt off the stage. After Oprah asked me the first question, it was several seconds before I spoke, my mouth slightly open. I shudder now, remembering how long it took for words to descend from my frozen brain to my parched mouth. I watched as I coached the women seated in the front row about how to eat alone in a restaurant. I was snippy with them, steering the conversation around to the power of personal retreats, trying to sell my book. My book cover briefly filled the screen.

I knew it during filming, and though I turned away from it in the intervening weeks, here was the truth: the outcome I wanted didn't happen. Oprah didn't say she loved my book or me. I was just a nervous woman flubbing an interview.

In the silence that filled my living room after the segment was over, before my friend Paula brightly exclaimed, "You were great!" and after another brief awkward hesitation before everyone chimed in, "Yes, yes, of course, you were great. You were on *Oprah*!" I came to understand that this interview was a turning point. Something had to change. It would take me years to enact this change. As I pushed snacks and wine on my friends and family and pretended to believe their kind words, all I was sure of was that it's not out there.

What I wanted wasn't in Oprah's hands or in hands of the people I loved who filled my house. The future I wanted didn't live in forcing and willing my reality to bend to my wishes, nor did it live in some gilded future only Oprah could deliver me to. It lived in my choices and actions.

I have so much compassion for the woman I was then. She wanted so deeply to be chosen, to have someone important tell her she mattered, that her ideas were good, that she was doing a worthwhile job. That she should believe in her work and herself. I didn't know how to choose me, how to love what I wanted even if I failed at it, or if no one with a national audience assured me I mattered. I only knew how to strain and seek approval.

About ten years after my *Oprah* debacle, I was talking to a writer friend about the business I had built around my work. She was still working in what I thought of as "the old model," which was to pitch articles, books, and speaking gigs and hope to get chosen. I knew this way well, as I had done it for fifteen years. She couldn't understand how I had made the shift to thinking of myself as a creative entrepreneur. I tried to break down the various moments of my shift and finally said, "One day I decided I didn't want to be at the mercy of anyone ever again. I decided I wanted to choose me and I wanted to, as much as I could, control my destiny." As corny as it sounds, when I heard myself say those words, power, desire, and self-regard came together in a whole new way. I looked back at how often I desired something but waited for someone else to make it happen, to tell me the right way to do something, to pick me. Choosing myself instead is scary—I self-published this book because I started to fall into wanting someone to pick me. If I did that, I knew it would undermine everything I'm advocating. I'm becoming by doing in a whole new way, and that's how we keep bothering.

Mindset Matters

I'm in my seventh-grade math class. I can feel the clammy plastic laminate of my desk and the weight of the oversized mauve-and-flesh-colored math book my teacher has handed me. He announces he is moving me up a grade. I sit up straighter and look around the room. No one else is getting the new math book but me. I feel so cool, recognized, chosen.

Only my teacher didn't have time to explain the new book. I would be doing independent study. He said something about what confidence he had in me and left me so he could help another student. "That's okay," I thought, "I'm smart. I'm special." I opened to the first page, wrinkling my nose at the book's industrial smell. I read the first couple of problems. Read them again. My eyes darted to my teacher. His back was to me. I looked at the page again. I had no idea how to do this kind of math. I didn't even know what kind of math it was. I willed my teacher to turn around and see my distress, but he moved to another group of kids who were playing paper football. I pretended to work. That's when I spotted the asterisk near the bottom of the page. I followed that asterisk to the back of the book where every single answer was laid out in a grid. I knew that cheating would only hurt me. What would my dad think if he could see me cheating? My stomach churned.

I did it anyway. I pretended to show my work. I even made a few answers wrong so I wouldn't arouse suspicion.

I whizzed through math for the rest of the year, copying answers and pretending to myself I wasn't. By the middle of the next year, eighth grade, I was failing math. I would never earn higher than a D in a math class again, even in Math for Artists in my freshman year of college.

Math was only the beginning. I became convinced that I was dumb, a fake, and a cheat in almost everything I did. I wanted to be a screenwriter and filmmaker; I wanted to work in theater, write novels, design a theme park. I was bursting with big dreams. I would try something—make a short film—and when it wasn't brilliant on my first try, instead of figuring out how to improve, I would quit, thinking, "That's all I got and it's not good enough." I'd start another project, always in search of something that would come easily. I was convinced that I couldn't learn how to do anything better.

Thankfully, smack-dab in the middle of my last big *why bother* time, I read the book that everybody had been raving about and that I had been dismissing as New Age crap. Halfway through the first chapter, I grew dizzy. I put the book down, closed my eyes.

"What's wrong, honey?" Bob said. His pillow rustled, and I knew he'd turned to look at me. I could picture his hazel eyes worrying about me.

"I just, I mean, I could do it all differently." I opened my eyes, bolted upright.

"What could you do differently?" He was using his "I better be careful" tone.

All I could do was wave the book at him. "Everything," I managed. He took the book, examined the cover.

"*Mindset*. What it's about?"

I struggled to explain what I was learning. It sounded too simple. I imagined Bob learning at five what I was learning now at close to fifty. "It's about how we aren't set in stone," I stuttered. "Our talents, our characters, our abilities aren't fixed. We can always learn."

He kissed me, rolled back over to read his book. "You're good at that, sweetheart."

But I wasn't. Not in the way I needed to be. Reading Carol Dweck taught me, for the first time, how to learn. Which in many ways is what bothering again is all about. She made me understand that desire was the starting point and could only flourish through the challenge of learning. The upshot of Dweck's research is "the view you adopt for yourself profoundly affects the way you lead your life. It can determine whether you become the person you want to be and whether you accomplish the things you value." We hold two views about ourselves, the fixed mindset and the growth mindset.

When we're in a fixed mindset, we assume our talent, our intelligence, and even our moral character is fixed and can't change much. Any success we experience is a confirmation of who we are, an affirmation of our inherent worth. As are our failures and mistakes. We learn to avoid taking risks and making mistakes so we can maintain our sense of being smart, being enough, and for some of us (me) feeling special. The fixed mindset is what convinces you there is no reason to bother because you can't do anything differently anyway. When I'm in a fixed mindset, I'm back in seventh grade, positive there is no way for me to learn, so I shrug and give up.

A growth mindset is the opposite. We understand our talent, intelligence, and moral character can be cultivated through effort. When we want something and go for it and it doesn't work or it's much harder than we thought it would be, instead of giving up or getting by or settling where we are, we brainstorm *how to learn*. We believe we can develop our talents and abilities "through application and experience." Nothing is fixed.

I know the growth mindset is talked about everywhere and that can make it easy to dismiss, but I believe without it, you can't sustain *what's next*, can't fully bring it to life. When a *why bother* moment comes along and you remember you can learn, you can change, you can handle what challenges are ahead, then you allow yourself to desire and decide, "Do I want it enough to take it on as a challenge? Do I want it enough to learn how to do it?" You can't do that from a fixed mindset.

You close off desire and becoming by doing without having any idea why. Shift your mindset in order to find *what's next*.

As you become more aware of your fixed mindset, how do you adopt more of a growth mindset?

- **Start to notice how and when you automatically assume you can't.** The fixed mindset can sound like, "That never works for me," "I have no time," blaming others for getting in your way, pretending you don't want something, never asking for help, or—maybe like me—defining yourself by your learning disabilities rather than getting curious about how to work around them. Notice how the fixed mindset shows up for you in thought and conversation.

- **Get enough sleep.** When you're sleep deprived, you don't even realize it. When the fixed mindset seems impossible to shift, first investigate how you are sleeping. Are you insisting the dog has to sleep with you even though she wakes up five times a night? Are you still having coffee in the afternoon? Reading your phone before bed? Without good quality sleep, you will have a very hard time getting your bother on.

- **Love the effort**. The fixed mindset loves to convince you that trying proves you're deficient, that the worst thing you could do is go all out and still fail. The growth mindset loves you to try. The growth mindset believes effort and bothering go hand in hand—you can't have one without the other. Remind yourself that making an effort, wondering, learning, and experimenting is where life comes rushing in.

- **Keep softening your self-judgment.** Each time you drop, soften, or decline to engage in bullying yourself, it's a huge boon to the growth mindset. Pay attention to what you want to learn, how you want to improve, what you want to try next, or whom you want to ask for guidance and decline to criticize yourself.

- **Replace fixed mindset thoughts with growth mindset thoughts.** Practice reframing your inner struggle in a forward-thinking "I can learn and grow" way.

Here are some examples of this reframe from members of the Oasis:

- **It's overwhelming!** Relax, it'll get done.

- **I don't know where to start!** Sometimes there are several paths in as opposed to one perfect route; just pick a reasonable place and start.

- **I don't yet know all the steps or what order to do them!** I trust that I'll know more once I reflect after the first step or two.

- **I don't have the time or money!** When I step back, I see there are ridiculously simple solutions to both of these challenges. I can do it.

- **I've messed up this type of thing before!** Yeah, but I've also succeeded,

> For more help with your mindset, come on over to jenniferlouden.com/whybother.

it's just that the negatives stick with us more strongly. And messing up means nothing in the end but a chance to learn. Plus, I can take care of myself.

- **Don't let the team at work see you sweat. Don't make an effort in front of them, or you won't look like a leader.** I want to be a vulnerable, authentic leader. I love watching tennis and I love the struggle a lot more than the winning. I will not pretend anymore.

- **If you were meant to do this, it would be easy. It's not easy, so you clearly aren't meant to do it.** Who says? Who made that rule? "Easy" is another way of saying "why bother?" Easy is boring. Bring it on! I love a challenge.

- **You've never made any money writing. Why do you keep doing it?** It would be wonderful to make money with my writing. I wonder what I could do to change that. I'm going to make a list and pitch that editor today.

- **You never finish anything.** That's an exaggeration and I decide what "finishing" means for me. I will use conditions of enoughness to decide my next steps.

Working with your mindset is about adjusting your attitude from "This is all I've got" to "Talent, intelligence, and charm are well and good, but what really matters is the effort I put in."

I see the growth mindset as a spiritual practice because it reminds me I am not my accomplishments and failures.

Adopting a growth mindset puts me back into the flow of life, into experiencing and growing. It takes me out of the small self who so badly wants to be somebody important and puts me back in touch with the wonder of experiencing life.

Go Ahead, Be a .... (Or Not)

Because of social media and the feeling that everything is for sale in our culture, I've found myself being genuinely interested in something—abstract painting, for example, or deepening my knowledge of Buddhism, or taking a more active role in climate activism—only to pooh-pooh my desire because it smacks of being trendy or clichéd. When you're looking for your way back into life, it's advisable to follow any trail that appears, cliché be damned.

I loved this passage in Alison Gopnik's essay "How an 18th-Century Philosopher Helped Solve My Midlife Crisis," in which she follows her wonder even if it is a Bay Area cliché: "I had always been curious about Buddhism, although, as a committed atheist, I was suspicious of anything religious. And turning fifty and becoming bisexual *and* a Buddhist did seem far too predictable—a sort of Berkeley bat mitzvah, a standard rite of passage for aging Jewish academic women in Northern California. But still, I began to read Buddhist philosophy."

But still.

I don't care if what interests you is on the front page of Goop, on the lips of every woman you know, is pinned on 20,000 Pinterest boards, or has its own hour-long infomercial. If it tugs at you, if it feels like one of your signature themes, please explore it.

Conversely, if you are being told by Pinterest or your book club or your friends what to care about and it makes you want to take a hundred-year nap, please heed that. You need not grasp at things that seem like a good idea or a should.

But what if you're interested in something—let's say it's pickling or restoring mid-century furniture or taking a retreat with a tantra sex master—but you wonder if the only reason it's calling to you is because it's on the tip of everyone's tongue. You don't know if doing _____ is coming from you, so you hesitate.

Two thoughts on this. First, since the life-giving kind of *why bother* is about being alive and loving without reservation, what form that takes in any given moment doesn't matter as long as it aligns with your values. Yes, it may turn into your job or vocation or important hobby at some point, but that's not what you're up to right now. Stay with the feeling of being alive.

Second, you may well be right, this is a dead end for you but not because it's all over Instagram or isn't a signature theme or isn't authentic for you but because you haven't yet settled down. You aren't wondering and desiring, you're grasping. If clues of what calls you, of what you desire, feel sticky, like they come with a chorus of "gimme gimme now,"

"Meaning arises from loving life, not from goals or narratives."

JULIO OLALLA,

THE RITUAL SIDE OF COACHING

settle down. Offer self-compassion to the parts of you that grasp. Gently notice your thoughts, feelings, and sensations while relaxing your jaw, your eyes, your shoulders. With tender curiosity, bring attention to what you're experiencing.

Meeting my pushy scrambling need to *do* and to *know* was how I finally stopped my long cycle of grabbing at the next thing. For so long, I believed I needed a project, an empire, a relationship, a bestselling book, even better baseboards in my bedroom as reasons to bother. But it was my clinging and my rushing that kept me away from life. And then when something would appeal to me, I'd dismiss it as a cliché. I was sure it had already been done, wasn't original enough, didn't matter, which panicked me and threw me into more rabid doing.

Clichés are meaningless. Experiments and wonder and self-trust and choosing are what signifies. When you feel like a cliché, the wisest response is to ask, "What do I want to try next?" Navigate by desire.

Spend Yourself

Don't be afraid of spending yourself on what you discover you care about.

Back when I lived on Bainbridge Island but before my life grew weary, I had tea with an old friend, Marta. She was visiting the island to see me and a college friend. She was a writer and actor, one of the most creative people I had ever known. I couldn't wait to settle in and hear everything she was up to.

I soon noticed something was off. She was saying the right words about the one-woman show she was writing and the edgy L.A. theater company that had invited her to join their ensemble, but something didn't feel right. It was like when you're streaming a show and your connection slows down and the words get out of sync with the actor's lips.

I put my mug down and shook my head. "What?" Marta asked. She sounded a little pissed.

I decided to be bold. After all, this was my dear friend. "I don't believe you really want any of that. You sound so dull." I held my breath, waiting for her to tell me I was full of it, that she knew exactly what she wanted.

She curled up over her tea and sighed. "God, you know me too well. I don't know what's the matter. But I feel like I'm going through the motions. Maybe I'm just too tired to want anything."

If this conversation took place now, I'd probably jump on the table and proclaim the life-changing magic of settling down. But Marta's life was sane. She wasn't into overdoing; she didn't flaunt being exhausted, and she took good care of her basic needs.

I made more tea and we talked into the afternoon. When we'd talked ourselves out and reached no new insights, and it was almost time for Marta to go to another friend's house, it slipped out of her mouth: "I've got one foot on the gas and one foot on the brakes. I'm afraid of spending myself. I get excited and then I hold myself back."

We looked at each other in that way good friends do when they know the truth has been spoken. She quietly added, "I'm afraid of going for it, of being great."

"That sounds like an exhausting way to live," I said.

She took her mug into the kitchen and stood looking out the window at the row of sunflowers that grew along my driveway. "I'm holding myself back from caring and it's exhausting me." She spoke to herself more than me. I almost didn't hear her. She shook her head slowly, gave me a long hug, and then got nose to nose with me. "I think we've discovered gold in them there hills!" Marta's life didn't look that different after our conversation, she kept working in theater, but she started enjoying herself more. She allowed herself to care and the inner experience of her life changed completely.

I've thought back to that conversation, both for myself and the women I work with, so many times. It's a delicate balance: taking care of yourself, gauging how much energy you have to spend, especially if you take care of someone who is ill or has special needs. When I was sick, I learned to hold myself back because I was so afraid of being in a situation I couldn't handle and not having a way to rest.

And when I was buried in the poop of *why bother*, I regularly gave up on myself, on even letting myself want to excel or try for greatness.

What's possible now? Are you holding yourself back from *what's next*, and is that exhausting you? Or as author and monk Brother David Steindl-Rast said to his friend, the poet David Whyte, when Whyte was lost in his *why bother* time, "You know that the antidote to exhaustion is not necessarily rest?"

"What is it, then?" Whyte asked.

Brother David said, "The antidote to exhaustion is wholeheartedness."

Is it time to spend yourself wholeheartedly, even to consider what greatness might look like for you? This is a challenging question because, for many of us, the idea of greatness leads to comparison, which plunks us back into "Why bother to do anything? It's all been done before and better." But when you declare that, you're strengthening the cramped self-limiting box of what is possible, narrowing your self-image, discouraging fresh insight, and falling back into the fixed mindset.

Comparing your greatness or idea of greatness to others assumes nothing you bring to the table is worthy or interesting. It's a question that places the focus outside of you, instead of centered in your desires. It's a capitalist stance that assumes what you do must make money or garner approval or it has no inherent value.

I prefer what one of my Oasis members said about greatness: "No matter if I am willing to be great or not, I am. We all are. The question is: 'Am I willing to share my greatness? Am I willing to step into my greatness? Am I willing to shape my life so it allows my greatness to come through?' I am. And it will take time to transform my life into one where my greatness can come through in the way I want it to. I can take small steps every day to get there, and I need to be patient on the way there."

Get Out of Your Own Way

As you move deeper into trying things, it's likely that you'll find yourself saying one thing and doing another. You'll be going in the opposite direction of what you say you want.

Let's say you want to meet someone, so you join the singles hiking club. But then you never go on an outing because your cat needs you to give her medicine or your hiking boots pinch. It doesn't matter that you could give the cat her medicine before you leave or you could borrow boots from your best friend. Until you surface the fear behind your conflicting actions, it will be impossible to do what you yearn to do. Fear drives us all to do things that directly compete with what we truly desire.

These are *not* things you take lightly or that make logical sense. These are the fears that make you shudder with embarrassment, make your palms sweat, your mind foggy. These are the fears you secretly believe no one else suffers quite like you. These fears may be very familiar, but *they still have heat*. You are truly afraid of these things happening even as your mind tells you to calm the hell down.

These fears are linked to what Robert Kegan and Lisa Laskow Lahey call your "big assumptions," beliefs that support your emotional immune system, protect your self-image, and make you feel safe even as they take you away from what you want. Going against these beliefs feels far too frightening because you're too exposed. On some level, you believe if you do what you say you want, you'll be annihilated. You'll experience a kind of death.

Let's look at a few examples.

Billy's Example

I want to care about:

- Painting and making art.
- Dedicating more time to painting.
- Finding a way to paint that excites me again, a style that is fresh and all mine.

What I do instead is:

- Say yes to more assignments at work when I don't need to.
- Say yes to attending more conferences.
- Spend the time I could paint looking at other artists' work and comparing myself.
- Copy other artists, then tear up what I made.

If I care about _____ , I'm afraid that _____
[your biggest hottest fears] will happen and that means
_____ [what's the worst possible outcome for you?].

- If I care about making art, I'm afraid that I'll paint for years and never get an exhibition and that means my life will feel pointless.

- If I care about making art, I'm afraid that people will see my art in my house and be fake-polite and that means I'm a loser and have nothing exciting to look forward to.

- If I care about making art, I'm afraid that I won't ever find my style, I'll keep copying others and that means I have no talent and never did and I will quit and my mother will be right: "better to never try than to fail."

Jani's Example

I want to care about:

- Starting a business that can provide for me in the last ten years of my working life and help me save enough to retire on.

- Creating a business I'm excited and proud of.

- Owning a business that makes a difference in transgender lives.

- Running a business that allows me to be more connected to people I can relate to and love taking care of; a business with real meaning.

What I do instead is:

- Complain about my current job.
- Take on more work so I don't have energy to work on my business.
- Spend all the money I make so I don't save so I won't have wiggle room when I retire or capital for my business.

**If I care about _____ , I'm afraid that _____
[your biggest hottest fears] will happen and that means
_____ [what's the worst possible outcome for you?].**

- If I care about starting my business, I'm afraid that I'll be suckered by every internet huckster and get completely overwhelmed and that means I'm an idiot.
- If I care about starting my own business, I'm afraid that I'll spend all my savings and never come up with a viable business and that means I'll have to work until I'm eighty.
- If I care about starting my own business, I'm afraid that I might leave someone in my community out and then get ripped a new one and that means I won't have a community anymore and I'll die alone.
- If I care about starting my own business, I'm afraid that it might be successful and then I will serve people I care about and what if they don't like me or think I'm radical enough? That means I'm a fraud, and that means I'm not who I want to be and I don't belong.

Kelli's Example

I want to care about:

- Writing. I want to be a great science writer.

- I want to care about helping people find their way back to facts, especially in rural and underserved communities.

- I want to care about making science legit and beautiful again.

- I want to care about helping change people's minds so they take action on the crises facing so many communities.

What I do instead is:

- Research, research, and more research.

- Work two minimum wage jobs and volunteer at my kid's school.

- Rage about the issues I care about.

- Read great science writing and despair.

If I care about _____ , I'm afraid that _____ [your biggest hottest fears] will happen and that means _____ [what's the worst possible outcome for you?].

- If I care about becoming a science writer, I'm afraid that I'll write stories with factual errors and be ridiculed on Twitter and that means I'm too lazy and stupid to be a science writer which means I'm worthless.

- If I care about becoming a science writer, I'm afraid that I'll put myself and my work first and neglect my kid and that means I'm selfish and a bitch.

- If I care about becoming a science writer, I'll afraid that my friends and family will get sick of me telling them depressing stats and they will ignore me and I'll lose respect for them and be all alone.

Erica's Example

I want to care about:

- Dating again, connecting with another human being intimately.

- Finding a best friend who wants to travel and enjoy life together.

- Having someone really know me and love me.

What I do instead is:

- Play computer games.

- Watch movies at home.

- Say no to invitations to parties.

- Not put up my profile on any dating sites.

- Not join the local singles meet-up group.

> **If I care about _____ , I'm afraid that _____**
> **[your biggest hottest fears] will happen and that means**
> **_____ [what's the worst possible outcome for you?].**

- If I care about dating again, I'm afraid that I'll betray my partner and I will forget what she looked like and smelled like and that means it's like our love never happened.

- If I care about dating again, I'm afraid that I'll discover I've forgotten how to be with another person and it will be so awful and that means there's no hope for me.

- If I care about dating again, I'm afraid that I'll fall in love and then people will be mad at me for moving on and that means I'm a terrible person for not grieving Ellen forever.

- If I care about dating again, I'm afraid that I'll relax my guard and I'll get hurt, and that means I'll get depressed again, I won't function and I'll end up back in the same hellhole as after she died.

Here's the thing: *we all have these kinds of fears around things we want but haven't acted on.* It usually takes some digging to get to the depth these folks found in the examples I've shared. I find most of us have to do this exercise a few times until we squirm and think, "Yep, that's my deep fear." Then by designing your nano-test (which you'll do next), you gather data that enables you to witness how your fears are ruling you and give voice to beliefs you perhaps didn't know had such a strong hold of you.

If you feel you aren't going deep enough, try reading what you wrote to a therapist, friend, or someone who knows you well.

I want to care about: _____

What I do instead is: _____

If I care about _____ **, I'm afraid that** _____
[your biggest hottest fears] will happen and that means
_____ **[what's the worst possible outcome for you?].**

Next, you test if your fears are as valid as part of you believes.

Take what you wrote for the last prompt (*If I care about* _____ *, I'm afraid that . . .*) and design a nano-experiment that tests your worst-case scenarios in a small, safe way and gives you data from which to ask, "Is this okay? Can I go further? Is it safe to do something different?"

You're testing your model of reality, creating an experiment that *could* cast doubt on your belief that it's not safe to take action on what you want. It's about witnessing your emotional immune system in action while taking a small, safe action that can expand the range of what you can comfortably do. What might these nano-experiments look like?

Erica decided to test "If I care about dating again, I'm afraid that I'll betray my partner and I will forget what she looked like and smelled like and that means it's like our love never happened." It suggested a possibility of testing and if she discovered it was true, she didn't think it would overwhelm her.

She decided to attend a meet-up of people interested in home brewing with the intention of looking for someone she might be attracted to. "I wasn't going to ask anyone out, but I wanted to see if I let myself look, let myself think about dating, if that meant my relationship with Ellen suddenly never happened." Erica reported her data to a friend afterward. "Thinking about dating, caring if I did it, actually made Ellen feel closer to me. I imagined laughing with her about how awkward I'd been. It's funny but just that little test made me look at my other fears a little differently. I think I'll be ready to ask somebody out soon and gather some more data."

Jani decided her first experiment would center on sharing her business ideas with her community and getting feedback. "I care so much about my business helping them, but I'm so afraid of not doing it right so I hide." Jani considered who she trusted to give her feedback on her idea. Designing an outcome that could lead her to question the validity of her beliefs would not be asking random people at a bar or people she knew to be fast to judge, but to ask the people she wanted to serve and whom she trusted.

She invited the people she'd chosen to her house. "I was shaking when I started talking but I led with talking about my big fears and asking everyone to be patient with me. Then I presented my three ideas and invited discussion using feedback questions a friend in HR had given me. What made this

"Don't apologize. Don't explain. Don't ever feel less than."

SHONDA RHIMES, YEAR OF YES

a safe, useful test was I paid attention to my thoughts about what it means to be part of the trans community and I outed them to the group. What I learned was how little they cared about that and how much they cared that I built a business that would actually work, for me first and the community second.

"What was huge about this for me was I understood what I wanted for myself mattered as much as being of service. I'd fallen into putting my community before myself to hide. That saved me so much time and wasted effort, not to mention not making any money!"

There aren't any precise rules to follow when designing your nano-experiment but keep in mind:

Safety

A safe experiment for Erica was to attend a home brewing meet-up with the intention of letting herself be attracted. A safe experiment would *not* be telling herself she had to ask someone out at the meet-up or be intimate with someone.

A safe experiment for Jani was running her ideas by people she trusted and wanted to serve. A safe experiment for Jani would *not* be deciding that the idea everybody liked was *it* and quitting her job.

Nano

Nano means small. If you tend to go big or go home, don't.

Action

You need to do something. Kelli wrote a short article about the possibility of ancient viruses being released by the permafrost melting and sent it to three science writers she respected for feedback.

Research

Your purpose is not self-improvement or behavioral change. It is to collect data about your beliefs, to cast doubt or learn its edges or how you might qualify it in the future. Kelli gathered the data that she was pretty good at research but needed to work on her narrative voice, and she also learned she wasn't depressed by her work but invigorated. Jani gathered data that her community cared about her more than her being a "good trans," which freed her up to get nitty-gritty about developing her idea to "actually make me some moolah!"

It's important you don't use the nano-experiment to try to disprove your fears or look on the bright side or force yourself to change your mind. Imagine yourself designing a test that will give you evidence one way or the other. Sometimes these nano-experiments will occur spontaneously, like when Billy was asked to join a painting process group and said yes. "Even though before I would have judged such groups as silly," Billy said, "I decided I would show up every week and make something I liked. I would not try to produce work I wanted to sell but only make things that pleased me in some way—texture or color or shape. Showing up week after week made me realize how little time I had ever devoted to learning what I liked or learning my craft. That turned out to be my nano-test and started big changes in how I experience myself as an artist."

The work of having a more spacious emotional immune system is never-ending. Every time you want to bother in a new way or your desires hit a bump, you'll probably find yourself having to examine your fears and then design an experiment or three to test them. But the good news is this tool works forever and allows you to move past the seemingly impossible choke points again and again. You don't have to get stuck ever again, at least not for long.

Reflect

Are you becoming more comfortable in the gap between where you want to be and where you currently are? What is helping you stay there longer?

How has "choosing you" gone thus far? Are you still waiting for your version of Oprah to choose you?

What does being satisfied feel like in your body?

Are you tempted to raise the bar on yourself and impersonate a robot or a cyborg? Can you look to nature for something else to emulate?

When, if at all, has the fixed mindset convinced you to hide, not try, or shrug off taking action on one of your signature themes?

If you asked someone close to you to describe your signature themes, what do you think they would say?

What has your body been telling you lately about what you care about?

What is one piece of data that, if you had it, might or might not expand what you think is possible to try? Would you consider designing a nano-test to gather that info?

Open the
door to your
beauty and
let others see
you caring.

_____

(10)

Be Seen

Hiding in Plain Sight

For most of my life, I wanted to be seen and admired, but I was afraid I wasn't good enough so I hid. My friend Laurie once demonstrated what I did to hide by fluttering her arms in front of her like a drunk octopus. "I really love you but you do this thing," Laurie said and her arms went all wild. "You distract people from you—sometimes you talk really fast or put yourself down. It's funny and cute but *it makes it really hard to see you.*" My cheeks flushed and I wanted to run away, but I looked Laurie in the eyes and said, "Yes, I see how I do that." Not only was I amazed I did not self-combust but I felt energized and relieved.

The next stage in getting your bother on is to let yourself *be seen.* This is delightful and comes easily to some of us, and then it's all about celebration and connection. And for others, this stage brings up so many danger signals, you might be tempted to skip it. But please don't. Open the door to your beauty and let others see you caring. How you do this is up to you—it may be intimate and quiet, or public like me writing this book. It doesn't matter one whit as long as you come out of hiding and let yourself be seen.

I've been in the public eye for nearly thirty years so I know you can absolutely hide in plain sight. I told myself I was an introvert and needed lots of time alone—which is true, but that wasn't why I often chose to be alone. It was because I didn't think I was worthy of being with other people.

When we don't let ourselves be seen bothering, we send ourselves the message we don't matter and that what we desire—and the very act of desiring itself—doesn't matter. We're telling ourselves, in effect, that it's not important to move forward with our lives.

We need a connection to other humans as much as we do food and water. Our brains need to interact with the world. We need human interconnection to be whole—which is why solitary confinement quickly becomes a form of torture. We might deny our need for others, resist it, have to work through trauma to repair our ability to connect, but without it, we can't thrive. *We can't bother when we are all alone*. We need to give our gifts to others.

When you let yourself be seen caring, moving forward, and desiring in the ways and time you choose, so much good can happen. When you share what matters to you—without hiding, downplaying, or puffing up—what you care about takes on a depth, a vibrancy, a concreteness. You gain energy, clarity, and perhaps refine or expand your *what's next*.

When you let yourself be seen *creating what you want* or *desiring and exploring*, you also increase your self-trust. You aren't looking for someone to say, "I approve," not at all. You're saying, "Hey, this is what I'm caring about, experimenting with, and I wanted you to share this. There is nothing weird or shameful about being in the *why bother* cycle. There's nothing bad about experimenting."

Of course, you might be *not* doing. You may be doing less than you have in years. That's extra-powerful to let others see because we live in such an overachievement-focused world. Even after retirement, people can be as frantic as ever about ticking items off their "bucket lists" and volunteering, which can be incredible if it's what you really want and you're present for the experience. I remember a successful actor friend who had been onstage since childhood saying about being pregnant, "It was the first time in my life nobody asked me what I'm going to do next. It was the first time I could rest because I was doing enough by making a baby." Being seen experimenting, resting, or doing less is to be seen trusting yourself—very inspiring indeed.

What does being seen entail exactly? You decide. It could be telling your friends you're training for a 5K. Joining a writing accountability group. Asking your partner to stop giving you advice but instead listen without commenting for fifteen minutes as you explore what's calling you. It could be saying, "I'm not ready to make a choice about what I'm doing next, still finding my desire" when people ask what you're up to. It could look like telling people you trust what your signature themes are and how much you care about them.

What being seen isn't is diminishing what you yearn for or are doing by apologizing. You don't say, "I'm doing one of those couch to 5K things but I know I'll never make it, or if I do, I'll be the last one across the finish line," or "I'm writing a novel but it's the worst. Total waste of time." Or "I know I should be clear and moving on with my life by now and I'm sorry I'm not." This is hiding in plain sight.

This doesn't mean you invite or accept opinions or feedback unless you genuinely are ready, and think carefully about whose feedback and what kind of feedback would be useful. Please don't do what I did and run around looking for someone to tell you what to do. I hired coaches and business consultants, consulted psychics, begged colleagues for their opinions. This isn't been seen or seeing yourself: this is looking for someone to rescue you or approve of you.

After I heard the title for my first book, *The Woman's Comfort Book*, but before I had done much work on it, I was on a women's weeklong canoe trip on the Rio Chama in New Mexico. We were a group of eight, all ages and occupations, and at twenty-seven I was the youngest by ten years.

We had a rest day on Abiquiu Lake. It was boiling hot, and we decided to go swimming. We found a sheltered cove, the shore made of a thick gray clay. The Pedernal, the flat-topped mesa Georgia O'Keeffe was obsessed with, towered in the distance.

I was about to wade in for a swim when Marcie, our writing and inner guide on the trip, grabbed a handful of mud and smeared it over her belly. "Okay," I thought, "we'll cover ourselves with mud, like at a tony spa." I should have known Marcie would have a much better idea. I'd never met anyone like her—both wise and wild, she spoke in myths and metaphor and didn't stop at the obvious or the surface. "No more worrying about my thighs," she shouted. "What shadow qualities are you ready to be rid of?" she asked the rest of us.

I grabbed a hunk of clay, held its heavy coolness. What did I want to be rid of? I smeared the mud on my belly, my muscular thighs, my neck. I thought about wanting my body to be different but after a week canoeing and living outdoors, I was in love with it. Instead, I blurted, "Wanting to be somebody important." I picked two handfuls of mud and threw these in the lake with a yip.

Marcie yowled coyote-like and we all flung ourselves into the spontaneous ritual. Clay smeared on our bodies, clay thrown in the lake, we barked our burdens: writer's block, illness, miscarriage, divorces, pain for the Earth, fear of dying. We dug our fingers into the slippery wetness, mounded ourselves into gray golems, roared into the sauna-dry air.

Finally, one by one, we collapsed on the riverbank. The only sound was our breathing and the lake lapping at our feet. The mud dried and pulled my skin taut. I licked my lips, tasted chalk. Vultures spun in a lazy circle above us. I closed my eyes.

After a time, Marcie said, "Time to bless and release." We waded into the lake in silence. With each splash of cool water, I imagined my doubts about myself, my need to be somebody, my fear I would amount to nothing washing away.

"Now what do you call in?" Marcie asked. "What do you appreciate about your unique lives, your gifts, your visions? What do you want?" The other women called out for things like freedom, a play produced, new love found, a repaired body after breast cancer. Marcie looked at me, waiting for me to speak. I almost dove underneath the water to hide but I surprised myself.

"I want comfort. Real comfort." I met Marcie's gaze. "I want comfort for us all."

Marcie swam closer. "Then this is what you must write, Jennifer. Your needs for comfort are everyone's needs. They are not self-indulgent, selfish, whiny, or self-limited," she said with the rhythm of a seer making a prediction. "They deserve to be spoken and tended to."

"I just want to know if I can do it." I took a big breath and the last chunk of clay fell off my chest. "If I can write this book. If it's a good idea." I expected her to say *of course you can*, to give me a pep talk, but Marcie was silent.

She cocked her head to the side like a scrub jay. "I can't tell you that." I wanted to slink away, hide in my tent. What a baby I was for asking such a needy question. "Nobody can tell you that," she added. "What matters is do you want it, are you willing to devote yourself to it? Devotion is your yes."

I couldn't help myself. "But do you think it's a good idea?" "What do you think?" she asked with a smile and then she waded out into the lake, leaving me to study the ancient red and white landscape where dinosaur bones lay. At first it embarrassed me. Where was my stamp of approval? Why didn't she tell me this was a great idea? I should have said nothing. But as I laid back on the water and half floated, listened to the water lapping at my ears, I became aware I'd shared something I wanted, and Marcie had heard me. She hadn't sold me a heap of false hope. She'd said, "If you care about this, do it." She saw me and told me that what mattered was what I wanted. I imagine now what a grin must have spread across my face, what a feeling of wonder and anticipation and faith that I was willing to try coursed through my body.

This is a big reason that women find the retreats I lead so transforming. I learned from Marcie we need to be witnessed but not rescued or advised. Participants make time for their desires by attending and then by declaring their desires to the other women in a space free of advice or comment—or even handing over the tissue box. Each woman has the space to get clear about what she wants, to let it become real to her, to hear it spoken in her voice with no one saying, "You can't" or "Who do you think you are?" or "Why do you think this time will be any different?" Instead, the group nods. "We believe in your right to claim this desire," they reflect with their loving silence. And as a woman owns her desires, those witnessing her wonder, "What do I want to create? To open my heart to?

To bother about?" These are not therapeutic forums; I am not a therapist and my retreats are designed to be forward-looking and with a generative focus, not a healing focus. I always use writing and other forms of creating to give us an anchor and because so often what helps someone ignite their *why bother* is being creative and reclaiming some aspect of their lost creative spirit, as well as making time for play. To share creating and playing makes it more real.

You'll remember back in the Leave Behind chapter we talked about leaving behind your identity, or at least whatever parts of it are outdated or getting in your way. As you move through this process, you are making a new identity that aligns with your new *why bother* story—and being seen by someone can help bring that identity alive. I started to become a runner when Jabe said, "You're a runner." People on my retreats start to claim or further develop fresh views of themselves when they say in exercises "I'm a writer" or "I'm creating." Saying it and having it witnessed doesn't make it so—but being witnessed can give what you want or who you want to be more weight and realness.

How do you re-create this gentle witnessing in your life? I've been part of formal groups, in person and virtually, whose purpose was to help each member articulate and then take action on our desires. Participants in the weekly Oasis, my online learning community, share desire retreats and desire declaration days. You can do this with a good friend or partner or church group. Each person states as clearly as they can what they want and then how they will use conditions of enoughness or some other approach to give shape and form to their desires. The other person listens closely, lovingly, and *silently*. That's the tricky part. We do so love to give advice or cheerlead, but the power of this practice is to hold our desires in company with no one butting in. There is a time and place for brainstorming, wise questions, and offers of aid but far too rarely is there time and space for desire to be witnessed.

Imagine you are in the lake with me. You stand tall with your shoulders back and your heart forward and tell me, "I care about _____. I will be devoted to it in these ways: _____. I am not demanding it be perfect or useful or profitable, only that I wonder and become by doing. I am not proving anything or expecting to arrive someplace where I am finally enough. I am listening and tending and making it up as I go along. I have nothing to hide about not knowing or not doing this fast or changing my mind. I do not need your approval or seek your opinion. I want to share with you what I'm up to."

I nod and together we lay back and let the water hold us.

Belong to Bother

Feeling cut off from other people can *cause* a case of *why bother* that's draining and blah and can intensify or prolong it. You need to connect and belong to people in ways you find personally meaningful. It's not about how much time you spend with others or alone. *It's about being seen and knowing you belong just as you are.* We need to share our experiences, to rejoice with others, to be recognized in our efforts, and loved for who we are.

Starting in high school, I believed I didn't belong—a common-enough adolescent thought, but one I never grew out of. By my mid-forties I was so lonely, I became worried for my health. I'd read the studies about how loneliness is equally as damaging as smoking *and* being sedentary combined. I became convinced I would die young because I had so little community.

I suspected my isolation was rooted in my fear of being seen for who I was, yet I was blind to how I could do anything differently. All my efforts to make closer friends or create more community seemed to falter after we had moved to Bainbridge. I finally gave up with a shrug. I blamed it on the "Seattle freeze," the idea that the Pacific Northwest is a difficult place to make friends, on working from home, on being a divorcée, on being a little intense, on anything but my choices and efforts, the story I was telling myself about belonging.

Like everything about that hopeless time, it makes me so sad to recall how convinced I was that nothing could be different. How sure I was that belonging, being seen, connecting with others in a way that fed my reasons to bother was all outside my control. But that's the devilish cleverness of the debilitating kind of *why bother*: our thoughts and then our actions prove its point. We can't see, until we do, that there is a way free.

"Stop walking through the world looking for confirmation that you don't belong. You will always find it because you've made that your mission. Stop scouring people's faces for evidence that you're not enough. You will always find it because you've made that your goal. True belonging and self-worth are not goods; we don't negotiate their value with the world."

BRENÉ BROWN, BRAVING THE WILDERNESS

I had lived on the island for close to fourteen years. Bob and I had gone out for a nice dinner to celebrate our anniversary. We ordered a plate of local oysters, each topped with a miniature flavored ice cap. Bob held an oyster up, studied it from several angles. "God, will you look at that?" He sucked the oyster free of its shell. He closed his eyes and sighed. I raised my wineglass to him. "Happy anniversary, my little foodie."

We ate the rest of the oysters, watched the tourists wander the four blocks of our miniature downtown, stopping to rearrange tired children in strollers and wipe the drips from their ice cream cones. It was seven in the evening but bright. Midsummer beauty.

"How was yoga today?" Bob asked.

"Good. Jen led a different sequence." I sipped my wine. "I saw Denise by the shoe cubbies afterward. She looked at me and then right past me." Bob studied the tourists. I knew he hated when I complained how nobody liked me. "Bob, that woman spurned me. I am not making this up. She said she wanted to be my friend, she told me she would throw a party for me with all her girlfriends, then she stopped talking to me."

He squeezed my hand, maybe a little too firmly. "I know she hurt your feelings. I don't know why. You don't either. You don't know what went on with her." I took a piece of bread with my free hand. Put it on my bread plate. Put it back. Bread made me itchy.

The waitress brought Bob a beer. I handed her the breadbasket so I wouldn't eat any. "I might like some bread," Bob said. The waitress quickly put the basket back on the table.

"I just want to not be so lonely," I said.

"I know, sweetheart. I know. Why don't we talk about something else on our anniversary?" But I wanted to keep whining.

There was a well-known writer I knew in the same way I knew so many people on the island—well enough to say hi, to know a few facts about her, and that was about all. She came into the restaurant with her family. We said hi as they were seated. The waitress brought our dinner and as we tucked into our wild salmon and braised greens, I watched her laugh with her family and wondered why we weren't friends. Last year she reached out to me to meet for coffee. I had been so excited, flattered, thinking this was a girlfriend date but she had only wanted me to sign copies of my books as gifts for her agent and editor. A few months later, she referred me for a plum speaking gig. Suddenly, I wondered if she had been making friendship overtures and I had missed them because I was so ready to be sure nobody wanted to be my friend.

I ate my fish and wondered if it was possible, just barely, that I had been the one dismissing and rejecting all kinds of friendships for my own weird reasons. I remembered all the offers to have a glass of wine with neighbors and how I'd always been too shy and skittish to say yes. Or imagined myself too special. I put my fork down. Too special, too busy, too weird. "My god, Jen, you have been taking yourself out before anyone could even invite you in." And why was that?

"Don't you like your dinner?" Bob asked. I realized I'd stopped eating and was staring out the window.

I shook my head. "No, I mean, yes, it's delicious. It's just that…" I looked at the writer again and then at Bob. "It's all good." I laughed, one loud guffaw that made several people look my way. It really was possible I was the one who had made belonging impossible, not anybody else.

That evening, I vowed to stop taking myself out of the running to have friends. I fessed up that I needed people. I needed to be connected to complete and sustain what I wanted to bother about. I needed to let myself belong and it wasn't predicated on me being successful or knowing what I bothered about. I just wanted to.

You may live far from like-minded people or family, be housebound with a disability or illness, suffer from anxiety or depression, or be someone's sole caretaker. And we are all being shaped by technologies that make it easier than ever to never leave our house. We can order dinner, stream a movie that won an Academy Award the day before, and text our nearest and dearest without getting off the couch. Which is all to say that loneliness doesn't have to be about your attitude, like it was mine, but it can still hurt your ability to bother again.

My anniversary dinner moment led to big changes. A year later we moved to Colorado and I was lucky enough to make several friendships there that changed how I see myself. But if I had not seen how I was isolating myself, and started right away, in our last year on Bainbridge, to say yes to my neighbor's invitations for a glass of wine, to stop saying, "Sorry, I'm too busy," and to prioritize keeping in touch with friends, I don't think I'd have the life I have now in Colorado. Because it's still far easier for me to be alone than it is to be seen and connected. I have to work at being seen.

Without other people, the creative process of living lacks vital energy. Something crucial is missing—both on a neuro-biological level and a soul level—and you will limp along or give up entirely.

Too often, our family, our friends, and our community overwhelm our desires, or we allow them to overwhelm us. I'm astonished by how many people, mostly women, that I encounter who still feel guilty about taking time for what they want. I sometimes feel like time has stood still for women in regard to feeling selfish, although I'm very heartened to witness less of this worry in younger women.

What I see women do to protect themselves is use isolation in place of personal boundaries. We may still deny ourselves what we want, we may still over-provide, but at least we can hide away sometimes. We isolate because it's easier to focus on what we want. This is not all bad—boundaries have to start somewhere and what's next for you needs time to become real to you—but at some point, you must learn to protect your time and energy while being connected to others.

I can see the faces of the women who recently attended one of my retreats. They're politely pretending to consider my idea that they must establish boundaries if they are to continue to explore *what's next*, and they must also connect with others and share their desires to complete the loop and keep the energy and insights growing. Jackie, her curls bouncing and her right foot working like a metronome, has a definite edge to her voice when she tells me and the group, "It's one thing to take this week for myself but it's not something most women can do except once in a long while. We take care of everybody, that's what we do. We can't stop." Most of the other women nod. I want to stand on my chair and scream, "No, no, no, that's not a fact, that's culture! Why are you still falling for that?" Which I know isn't fair, as culture determines so much of what we think and do, yet it feels like so many of us still accept what it means to be a woman without asking what aspects of the current cultural definition fit us. It's almost as if we want an identity that makes us indispensable to other people's needs because then we don't have to do this hard work of finding our own *why bother*.

What I heard underneath Jackie's protest is a longing to keep making this space for her desires, and I heard fear. Fear that her desires weren't worthy of such time and attention, weren't worthy of inconveniencing her husband or her son or her religious community. That they wouldn't amount to anything. Better to do what she knew she was good at, better to fit the mold of a good woman, than to risk.

Journalist Brigid Schulte wrote an article that went viral about women not creating great masterworks because they never had the time. She said, "I wonder if that searing middle-of-the-night pain that, at times, settles like dread around my solar plexus may not only be because there's so little

Create Your Own Community

Consider gathering a group of people for a limited period—say for three months, meeting every two weeks, in person or on a videoconference platform like Zoom. The purpose of the group would be to give each person a few minutes to be listened to without being interrupted about where they are in their *why bother* reinvention. The only rule is no advice, no problem solving, no commenting, not during the circle or later over tea or carpooling home.

For introverts, you might do this with one or two buddies. Email or phone works too.

A caution about being seen on social media: the connections and support we get on the internet can be lifesaving and life-enhancing, but in general, social media—Facebook, Twitter, Instagram, LinkedIn—are not always fulfilling ways to share what's happening in our inner worlds. We can be lectured, told to buck up, or be ignored entirely. It's a terrible feeling and not one you want to set yourself up for right now. Instead, reach out to individuals, whether in person or via text or messaging service. It's a more tender way to take care of yourself.

unbroken time to tell my own untold stories, but because I'm afraid that what may be coiled inside may not be worth paying attention to anyway. Perhaps that's what I don't want to face in that dusky room I dream of." And then she concluded, "What would happen if we decided women deserved the time to go to their dusky rooms and stay awhile at the kitchen table? What if we all decided to visit more often, drinking a quiet cup of tea with ourselves, listening to the coil of stories as they unspool, knowing they have value simply because they're true? I'd love to see what happens next."

Connected to Oneness

I've been a spiritual seeker since I was a small child. I've been a Southern Baptist, taught myself meditation and yoga from Ram Dass's book *Be Here Now* at twelve, explored lots of New Age stuff in L.A. in the early '80s (including a weird brand of Buddhism akin to the Christian prosperity gospel), and was in a women's goddess nature ritual group for a few years. When Lilly was born, I joined the local Unitarian Universalist church but when we moved to Bainbridge, I tried to be an Episcopalian. I'm sure I've forgotten a few of my spiritual forays. What I always came back to, what threaded through all my spiritual wandering, was whatever helped me remember my inherent goodness and my connection with oneness.

In all those wildly different traditions, I experienced feeling myself as a separate entity dissolve. It happened in a pristine Canadian lake, after taking part in a traditional Indigenous sweat lodge, no separation between the stars, the water, and me. Chanting in kirtan. During ecstatic dance. Hiking in the redwoods. Certainly during meditation. I felt held by love and a part of everything. I treasured these moments as some of the most luminous and meaningful of my life, yet somehow I never connected them as an antidote for feeling lost. My story line that I repeated—that I wasn't allowed to bother again because I had made too many mistakes—would overtake me and the mystical oneness would become a pleasant memory. I didn't realize I could rely on these moments of profound connection to help me find the river of my life again.

Then I was on a business planning retreat with a group of friends when life or god or whatever it was decided enough was enough. It was time for me to get the message, connect the dots, and know once and for all how things really are.

We set up our yearly retreats so we each took the "hot seat" for about ninety minutes, presenting what we wanted to work on in our business. Then the group brainstormed and coached us so we emerged with new ideas and fresh perspectives. It worked beautifully because everyone was a skilled coach, several were longtime spiritual practitioners in different disciplines, and we'd known each other for years. It was impossible to hide.

I don't remember what grand plans I presented to the group about my business ambitions that year but I'm sure they were grand. Back then I believed I needed to make something giant to get me out of my funk. I didn't get very far into describing my world domination strategy before an intense, almost painful, kind of joy overtook me. I closed my eyes and laid my head back on the couch. I was suddenly engulfed in that numinous oneness. It was like walking into a vast cave, only instead of darkness this was all light. I was present but also everywhere. It was intensely familiar but also completely new.

"Wow," I stuttered. "Something is happening."

Eric asked gently, "What are you aware of?"

I couldn't find words for what I was inside of. It had no end and no beginning. It was so alive. It was me but not me. I settled on saying, "It's here," and then, "I can't leave it."

Mark said, "We're here. We've got you." I still find it astonishing how immediately everyone knew to let me go with what was happening and how perfectly to support me. For me, being witnessed surrendering to whatever was happening made all the difference. I'd never melted into oneness with others—I'd always been on a solitary or silent retreat or alone in nature, people nearby but not with me.

And every time I had experienced this oneness, I had freaked out and held myself back a little bit. Tightened up. Came back too soon. But on that damp gray March morning, with my friends around me, I surrendered my striving, separate, needy, worried, never-enough self more than ever before. To what I surrendered, I have no idea. Was it random neurons firing or a direct experience of god or the true nature of love or awareness itself? No idea. But it changed everything.

As I gave myself more and more to the waves of exhilaration and joy, and as my friends coached me to relax and laughed along with me, a cold dry stuckness at my core, a stony pit I had been aware of since adolescence, unknotted. It didn't disappear but it became part of the vastness. Welcomed. Seen. Loved.

I emerged slowly. We laughed, I ate some chocolate, everybody else went out for a walk and I fell into a deep sleep. I dreamed wonderful dreams that I couldn't remember except to know, when I awoke, that this time I would not forget the wholeness and I would never believe again I wasn't worthy of bothering. Never.

I believe there is a oneness that holds you and is always here for you, and which makes up the core of you. I believe letting that oneness see you in all your mess and glory, in all your lostness and foundness, is the ultimate belonging.

You've recognized oneness when you held a newborn baby, her eyes still filled with belonging. You've felt it when your mother took her last breath. Immersed in a summer evening listening to your local symphony made up of your neighbors as the musicians became something bigger together in the music. You knew it reading Diane Ackerman or Hafiz or Wendell Berry or the gospels or the Koran, the words ringing through your chest like you were a gong being struck with a mallet of eternity. You recognized it when you dissolved during sex, touched color to a canvas, watching a hummingbird's tongue pump pollen into her body. On and on, generous beyond imaginings, this enduring love offers itself to us.

But, and there doesn't have to be a but, but if there is, it might be "But the oneness didn't last." It glimmered for a minute or a day or a week and then you had to come back, sit in a boring meeting, wipe a bottom. Or it scared you, shook up how you see yourself. Too big, too much. Or you dismissed it because you're not religious. Or because no one else seemed to know what you were talking about.

This is a very common reaction. We either want to dismiss what we've experienced or cling to it as proof we are special and wholly changed for the better or focus on getting more. We insist everything is love as we fall back into our old ways of not caring—because who needs to care when you're one with everything?

What we want to do instead is use the knowing to help us stay connected to life in every moment. To *be* the river of life without forcing and without holding back. Oneness never leaves us. It is the blessing in *why bother*. It is the presence in the air when a group of people pray or meditate with great sincerity. It's the breath you just took. It's always here.

Whatever it is, all it wants is for you to turn toward it, to let yourself be seen by it. Perhaps this is why a personal relationship with a god is so healing: we let ourselves be known by love, the most gnarly and despised parts of ourselves and the most beautiful, our gold, our power, our luster along with our shattered twisted parts.

Turn toward that which never leaves you and which you cannot leave, even if you have no experience or no name for

"Even if I don't
see it again—
nor ever feel it
I know it is—
and that if once
it hailed me
it ever does."

MARIE HOWE, "ANNUNCIATION"

it, let alone a belief in it. This is not about belief or religion or even spirituality. It is about faith there is love in the world and that you are not alone. Think about it: gravity holds you to the Earth. Oxygen keeps you alive. The food you eat is grown and harvested by hundreds of people and processes. The people who have taught you, inspired you, held you when you cried, the woman who held the door open for you at the store yesterday: that's love, that's support, that's what you can lean back on.

Imagine yourself standing before what you hold sacred, imagine leaning back on all that supports you without having to do a thing, and all that love saying to you, "I see you."

You are seen. What you want and who are you is enough. Open to this truth.

No forcing, no holding back.

Confessions

My dad was diagnosed with pancreatic cancer when he was eighty-four. He was lucky to get the best treatment available. He endured two years of heavy-duty chemo without complaint and was still able to enjoy his life. We knew he would die, there was never any question, because of his age and because the tumor was inoperable. The two years we had together were precious, and I thought I was prepared for him to die. I talked a good talk about "looking death in the eye"

and "you could only live well if you could face your death."
Growing up with an older dad, rare for my generation, we'd
talked a lot about his death.

Jump ahead with me. Dad has been gone almost three
years, having died of a heart attack brought on by the chemo.
Chris and I have split up, and I've met Bob. It's a midsummer
evening. Lilly is with Chris, Aidan is with his mom, and Bob
and I are lying in bed.

Even though it was past ten, there was still a pearly
glossy light in the sky. I had left the roller blinds up so we
could watch the day's last light fade. Bob held me, his chest
hair springy like crabgrass under my cheek. He smelled like
Dr. Bronner's peppermint soap. The dogs snored in their beds.

"I love you, baby," Bob said.

"I love you too."

He heard something in my voice; he already knew me
that well. "What's the matter?" I could feel him ever so sub-
tly tense. I patted his chest, sat up. "It's nothing to do with us,"
I said. Could I tell him? I needed to tell him, to tell someone.
If I didn't, I wasn't sure I could go on.

I see myself walking into Mom and Dad's house. Their
neighbor Joyce is moving toward me like she's on a moving
sidewalk. She kisses my cheek, "I'm so sorry, Jennifer," and
I am thinking "You've never kissed me before" and "Why
were you here for his death and I wasn't?" Joyce on her moving sidewalk passes me and I am on my own conveyer being
taken to my dad's body. The difference between an hour and

"I believe that telling our stories, first to ourselves and then to one another and the world, is a revolutionary act."

———————

JANET MOCK, REDEFINING REALNESS

a half ago and now, the difference between when I got on the
plane from Italy a week ago and now, coalesce into a distance
that I cannot cross.

"Honey?" Bob asked.

I'm back in my bedroom with Bob. I laid back on my pillow.
Pulled the covers up to my chin because I was chilled. "I need
to tell you about Dad." I watched the big Douglas fir fade into
darkness outside the window.

"I'm here," Bob said.

He's here. I'm here.

"I haven't told anybody this story." I take his hand. "I was
in Italy when Dad had his heart attack, visiting Chris on the
show," I begin. Chris had been traveling around the world for
four months shooting a reality TV show, and when my work
took me to New York, I booked tickets for Lilly and me to go
from there to meet in Milan so at least we would see him once
during the duration.

"I know that, honey. You didn't know he would have a
heart attack."

"Here's what I didn't tell you." I do not look at him. "My
cell didn't work in Italy so I gave my mom the number of the
production company. But she didn't have the right phone
number. When I gave her the number, she tried to say it back
to me and I cut her off midway. I cut her off because I was in
a hurry. If I hadn't, she would have been able to call me right
after he had the heart attack, not two and a half days later
after someone else finally tracked me down. I would have

gotten back in time to say goodbye." I can see myself standing
in the kitchen talking to Mom and thinking she's being overly
cautious and I don't have time for this.

"Even after I knew, I didn't come home right away. Bob, I
didn't leave Italy for another day and a half. I went to Venice
with Chris and his crew, instead of going to Milan and straight
home from there. Chris and Lilly and I went out to dinner
that night. My dad was dying and I was eating pasta." I want
him to say something, to hug me. I want to move to him but
I'm frozen. The room is dark with silence, even the dogs have
stopped snuffling. I plunge on. Might as well get the clean-
swept feeling of a confession even if, I realize now, it means
losing Bob's respect.

"When Lilly and I got back to the island, I didn't go straight
to the house. I went to bed. I went to bed and I slept. I didn't
go to Mom and Dad's, even though I said I would. And when
I woke up," I shuddered, gripped the blanket with both hands,
"I did laundry. I started a load of laundry and took a shower
and I shaved my legs." I wanted to scream the next part but I
could only whisper it.

"And when I got there, when I finally got there, Dad was in
a coma and when I asked when he had stopped responding,
all my sister knew was it had been in the last hour." I rolled
away from him. "In the last hour."

Bob tried to pull me to him then, to stroke my hair, but I
pulled away, threw the covers off. I wanted to be alone and I
wanted him to tell me I was a monster. "I didn't even stay an

hour, Bob. I told my sister and my mother that I had to go buy printer ribbons so Lilly could print her paper for school on Monday. I left and then he died." Finally, I rolled over to face him. "I was out buying printer ribbons when my dad died."

He cleared his throat. "That's so tough." I held my breath. Would he tell me it's no big deal? That I was in shock and that's why I made such stupid choices? That I loved my dad so much I couldn't bear being present when he died? Maybe he would blame Dad for not waiting for me to be there with him, which would make me break up with him because no one could say anything bad about my dad, but still, it would be nice. How dare Dad do that?

"There's only one thing I don't understand, Jen," Bob said slowly, working something out in his mind. "You told me about when you confessed to him in the middle of the night the stuff about smoking pot at school and lying to him." I swallowed. I'd told Bob that before? I'd blanked that little spot of shame right out. "How could you have stayed only an hour after you arrived if you also talked to him in the middle of the night?"

I covered my mouth. Two images struggled for supremacy in my memory: me pulling away from Mom and Dad's house in the orange Volvo, Lilly in the back seat, going to buy printer ribbons and me lying on the floor of the living room in the shadow of Dad's hospital bed, listening to the rattling whoosh of his breath, then standing over him, confessing everything I had been too chicken to tell him when he was conscious.

"I did leave to get printer ribbons, but it was the next day." I tasted copper and realized I had bitten the inside of my cheek. Bob moved to hug me, but I held up my hands. "But so what? That doesn't mean anything. I still didn't get home. I still left." I rubbed at my mouth. "I still wasn't there. At the last moment."

"I'm sorry, darling. That's really tough."

I wanted to leave him and go sleep in Lilly's room, bury my nose in her teenage tang. I wanted to get up and drink tequila at the kitchen counter. I almost suggested, "We're dating, let's have some fun." But instead, I screwed up my courage and asked Bob the hardest question of all.

"Do you think Dad didn't want me there? When he died?" There it is. The real confession. "People say that we have control over when we die." I let out a shuddering breath—the kind a child lets out when she is finished sobbing although I had yet to cry. "Why did he die when I wasn't there?"

"I don't know." He gently moved me around so he could spoon me to him. We fit together like long-lost puzzle pieces. "I didn't know your dad and I so wish I had, I will always wish I had, but from everything you've told me he was not the kind of man who would ever do anything like that to his girl." He kissed my hair. "I don't know that, but I do know he loved you with all his heart."

I nodded, a tiny nod. After Bob fell asleep, I wriggled free and went downstairs to lie on the couch and stare at the patterns on the ceiling made by the trees and the porch light my neighbor Valerie left on when her husband was out of town.

She was afraid of the dark. My dog Luna came down and curled up in the crook of my knees. I lay still and wondered at how I almost felt forgiven.

Telling Bob was not about leaving behind my guilt but being witnessed in having it. In telling Bob, I opened the door to my freedom. In time, I would forgive myself. I would stop believing that I had to suffer for my choices. I'd confess again, years later, this time to my sister, and she would say, "I just figured you were scared." And so I was.

Reflect

How might you connect with others and be seen in a way that helps you continue to thrive?

What are you afraid to be seen wanting, taking action on, moving ahead with? Can you design a nano-experiment and gather data about this fear?

Are any of your shadow comforts or time monsters a substitute for connecting and being seen? What might be more fulfilling even if it means risking being disappointed or rejected?

Who (living or dead) might you think you are betraying by being seen growing, flourishing, caring?

Who could you be helping by being seen growing, flourishing, caring?

You will always have to begin again. Embrace this truth and you'll always be able to get your bother on.

———

Conclusion

Always Begin Again

When Am I Bothering?

- When you wake up grateful more often.

- When rest is not a four-letter word.

- When not knowing is a territory you yearn to return to, even if you pack a trailer's worth of supplies first.

- When you stop asking everybody and their life coach for advice until you first listen to yourself.

- When a day, a project, a meeting, or a relationship hits a pothole and you take it as sign to get curious.

- When you keep your ear tuned to the deepest current of your desires.

- When spending yourself on something you care about is not a recipe for burnout, but a rebirth.

- When your fear of not being original, of wasting time, of looking like a fool, of being skewered on social media wilts in the face of your hunger to grow, to experience, to create.

- When you accept your limits as a container in which you can create extraordinary beauty.

- When you trust you can handle what life brings, and that has nothing to do with getting things right or being successful and everything to do with never giving up on yourself.

- When you hear the sounds of your hamster wheel grinding away and, without further ado, you step off.

- When you catalog your complaints to discover what's calling you next.

- When your chronic illness or debt or grief pushes your face into the carpet and when you have a modicum of energy, you push back and call out for help.

- When you look at your success not as golden handcuffs but as a foundation for reinvention.

- When you don't ignore entrenched power, institutional racism, and sexism, and you don't fight them alone.

- When you know the mind likes things done fast, but the soul does things on its own timetable.

- When self-care and collapsing into numbness are two very different choices.

- When *what's next* is an unfolding love affair, a becoming.

- When you can express your anger and rage more of the time.

- When you are 100 percent certain the life you have and the life that will unfold for you is worth showing up for.

- When being comfortable with discomfort has become a skill you rely on and even revel in.

- When you refuse—more of the time—to live as anything less than one radiant face of aliveness.

- When you are writing a new story every day.

- When you accept that the cycle of *why bother* will begin again, and instead of fighting it, hating it, blaming yourself or someone else for doing something wrong, you take a deep breath, or twenty, and settle down.

- When you trust your next round of becoming is already happening.

How to Remember

Distill what bothering looks and feels like, as it's best for you. The aim is to give yourself a concise vibrant snapshot of the *act* of bothering. Now that you know how you want to bother, give yourself a way to remember.

When you're caring in a way that's deeply satisfying, calm, self-trusting, energized, alert, open to wonder, and tuned to the growth mindset, how would you describe that kind of bothering? Play with any of these questions to get started:

- If your style of bothering were a color, what color would it be? *Peacock blue, lemon yellow, fire-engine red?*

- What mode of transportation? *Hiking boots, bullet train, Porsche convertible, donkey . . .*

- What geographic location? *It can be an imaginary place, made up by you or someone else.*

- What character from a movie, TV show, or book is similar to you in how they bother?

- Might there be a poem, a quotation, a line of scripture, a sutra that encapsulates your preferred way of bothering?

- If you created a small living library of resources to remind you how you want to open to life, what would you include? Think music, people, places, books, art, food, weather . . . anything goes.

What are five actions you take when you're bothering your way? Mine are pausing (to feel, to settle, to welcome), moving my body (stretching, dancing, walking around the block), journaling (in the form of a cluster map or dialogue with various parts of myself), disrupting a routine, and connecting with people by phone or in the flesh.

Play with distilling what helps you remember into something you can make into wallpaper for your desktop or stick on your bulletin board or carry with you to read when you're waiting in line. What will help you remember how you love to get your bother on?

Always Begin Again

One warm July afternoon at the Mabel Dodge Luhan House in Taos, New Mexico, I was leading a writing retreat and talking about the power of "begin again," how having the self-compassion to start over—whether you stopped or something stopped you—is the most helpful idea and one of the most difficult to allow ourselves. What we often do is dodge the fact we stopped, try to figure out why we stopped, wait for our life circumstances to change, or make a complicated plan for how to never fall off the wagon again—and stick to it for a couple of days and then feel defeated again.

Ruth took me aside after the class. "There's something I learned in the Benedictine tradition, Jen, that you might like. 'Always we begin again.'"

I rocked back and forth in my Birkenstocks. "Always?"

"As in have mercy on yourself. You'll always lose your way, give up, doubt yourself. It's inevitable. So don't be surprised by it. Always begin again."

Always. What a miraculous word. Stop expecting yourself to be steady, consistent, uniform, perfect, or otherwise robot-like in anything. You will always have to begin again—and that includes bothering.

Why bother will always have two sides, two faces, two polarities—ignore or take stock; stay stuck or decide what to leave behind; shrug or wonder; distract or settle; deny or desire; freeze or become by doing; hide or let yourself be seen; freeze at the first sign of *why bother* returning or always begin again.

The nature of life necessitates you continually reckon with what you care about, that you ask when you need to, "What's the point?" The process is never over. Not that there aren't long stretches of time when you don't think about what you want or why you care. But please don't assume that when you do ask, when you do question, when you find yourself back in a rut, something has gone terribly wrong. And please don't assume if you've come to the end of this book and you aren't 100 percent vibrant, clear, and on fire about *what's next,* something is the matter.

You've been finding the desire to discover. Not pinning your future down. Not making a grand plan. Not achieving or even figuring much out. You've been dipping and floating and enjoying the river of life. And just by reading these pages, you've done an awesome job.

How do I know? Because I have encountered so many people, as have you, who aren't willing to even look at what it means to care, to engage, to live again. Maybe you were one of them. Maybe you are still half thinking that's the best choice. Give up, coast, stay safe, who cares? But I don't believe for a second that having read this far, you continue to hold on tight to the story that there is nothing satisfying ahead for you.

An odd assortment of choices and a considerable sprinkle of luck and privilege pulled me back into life. I could have never guessed I would end up where I am today, and I'm not speaking about my career or house or anything tangible. It's the inside I'm proud of. It's the strong faith I have that I won't ever give up on myself or on life again. I hope you have a smidge of that as well. If not, you can always begin again.

I often run by myself on mountain trails. There are mountain lions around, and while the chance of being attacked is minuscule, I need to be alert. One day, huffing up a mountainside, I thought I heard an animal following me in the trees. I knew it was most likely snow melting or a deer, but it made me think about what I would do if a big cat jumped on me.

Then the strangest thing happened: I heard a loud breathy exhale as if a very large animal had breathed directly into my right ear. I whirled around, ready to fight, positive I was going to have to wrestle a mountain lion. I looked up into the trees, then all around me, turning around and around on the trail like a dog chasing her tail. But there was no animal. I was completely alone.

But what was it? Maybe my foot slipping on a rock? I started running again, shaking my head, and then I started laughing so hard that I had to stop. No, I wasn't laughing because it's silly to imagine I could fight off a mountain lion. I was laughing because I loved life so much I would want to try. The woman who wanted to be done so badly she imagined slipping over the side of the ferry had become the woman who would fight the mountain lion her overactive imagination had conjured. Hell yes, I knew how to bother. I took off running and singing, "I love you! I love you!" I was singing to everything: the trees, the mountains, my family, Bob, my body, my heart. I was singing to life.

We stay on the lousy side of *why bother* when we work against life. I worked hard at giving up. I worked so hard at fighting against caring again, against coming back to life. What a lot of effort I put into being unfulfilled, into being envious, isolated, judgmental, and self-doubting. Funny how we do that. But we can learn to do it differently. That's what amazes me most about being a human: our ability to learn, and in learning, to change everything about how we perceive our lives. We can open to life even when terrible things have happened to us or have been done to us, even when we are in the midst of ongoing grief and hardship. And from this place of openness and optimism, who knows? Perhaps we can make it possible for others to have the opportunity to bother about what they desire.

Bothering doesn't fit a timetable. Writing your new story doesn't either. Don't let anybody bully you into hurrying this transition. Trust that you have or will cross a threshold. Trust that life is rising in you, that you're creating *what's next* based on what you desire. Are you feeling more engaged? More engrossed? Are you wondering more? Stretching? Venturing past the known? Testing your assumptions? Trusting yourself with self-compassionate grit? Minding the gap? Remembering you matter? Letting yourself settle down? Then you are bothering.

Where does all this take you in the end? What's the payoff? The point?

The point is caring.

The point is loving life again.

The point is when you die, you're not wondering who you could have become, what you could have experienced, who you could have loved.

Why bother, it turns out, is your ace in the hole, your compass, your mantra, your touchstone, your trickster question, jumper cables for your soul. It's the ninja move you can pull out whenever you need it. *Why bother* will always be there to help you discern, to tickle you to look ahead, not in a greedy, grabby way but in a grinning, desire-filled way.

Thank you for being courageous and thank you for allowing me to join you in this adventure. Thank you for being willing to go into your lostness, blahness, apathy, and despair, and search for your *what's next*. It matters in ways you will never know. Thank you.

Acknowledgments

USUALLY LOVE WRITING the acknowledgments but because this book took twelve years to incubate, I'm terrified I've left out scores of people. My apologies in advance for my faulty memory.

Big thanks to the pros at Page Two. You each made it possible for me to choose myself and publish a book that is better than what I could have done with a traditional publishing deal. I've had great publishing teams at the big publishing houses, but you all rocked my book with your care and attention to detail. Amanda Lewis, your editorial guidance was brilliant. Thanks for Bananagram-ing my missing and blind spots and for your fantastic subtitle help. Jesse Finkelstein, thanks for your patience over my year of deciding to make the self-publishing leap—and I'm so very glad I did. Peter Cocking, your art direction made my ideas stand out. Annemarie Tempelman-Kluit, thanks for all the brainstorming and expertise. Caela Moffet, none of this would have happened

335

without your attention to detail and ditto to Crissy Calhoun for your excellent copy edit. Thanks to Jennifer Lum for design help and Lorraine Toor for getting the book seamlessly into the world.

To each of my Oasis members, you were instrumental over the years in helping me develop the ideas in this book, as are the women who have attended my retreats and workshops over the last three decades. Your brilliance, rigor, and curiosity pushed me to learn, and I will be forever grateful.

To the people who sent me stories or gave me ideas or support to help me understand why to bother, I am so grateful. Char Brooks, Randi Ragan, Carol-Anne Savage, Terry Jordan, Jeanne Ambrose, Sarah Flick, Lori Jordache, Paula Trucks-Pape, Petra Duguid, Tammy Roth, Caitlin Faas, Elaine Fourie, Laura Roman, Cheri Honeycutt, Julie Green, Rachel Ford, Dana Childers, Jennee Harmuth, Jessica Scott, Rhianne NewLahnd, Wendie Donabie, Alexis Neely, Cathy Standiford, Alison Luterman, Marilyn Yohe, Monica Miller, Barbara Lee Johnson, Marianne Oude Nijhuis, Christine Herman, Jen Milette, Nicola Mendenhall, Jennifer Nash Humphrey, Linda Mason, Susan Kimball, Lynne Tolk, Nancy Fries, Allison Leonard, Christine Rosas, Tracy Muklewicz, Jennifer Cole, Catharine Bramkamp, Kate Mayer Mangan, Jaime Fleres, Amy Oscar, Michele Ceres, Carole Downing, Andrea Scher, Kelly Lee Perry, Jean Starr, Nisha Mead, Lise Richards, Susan Hyatt, Cindi Brown, Finka Jerkovic, Nicola Newman, Kasmin Kaneko, Marie Hood, Wendy Moore, Beth

Bruno, Roni Walker, Celia Beaumont, Cecelia Fresh, Elana Baxter, Leigh Juska, Carol, Elaine W., Rebecca Alder, Martha Miltich, Melissa Capers, Linda Mosedale, Suzanna Steenbergen, Leigh Lawhorn, Dawn Friedman, Kimberly Ramsey Stromgren, Ren Powell, Elizabeth Barbour, Gwen Fox, Terri Jackson, Heather Hall, Jen Duchene, Mimi Seeley, Dana Stewart, Laura Theimer, Laura Davis, Jill Holman, Roberta Shine, Randall Snelson, Kim Bain, Faye Harvin, Robin Murphy, Chris Zydel, Melanie DewBerry, Beth Thompson, Theresa Jarosz Alberti, Lisa Wells, Shawna Atteberry, Janet Mar, Molly Remer, Ed Stanford, Jennifer Ross, Kathi Parker, Mindy Stern Meiering, Barb Klein, Pam Bustin, Rachel Egan, Laurie Wagner, Julie Daley, Kenyatta Monroe-Sinkler, and those of you who wished to remain anonymous.

To all my teachers, I am grateful every day I have the privilege of learning from you.

To my wonderful Prospect friends, how lucky I was to stumble into your clan! Jen Paris and Kelly Hendershot, Barb and Steve Wolfe, Susan and Keith Jaggers, Kimberley Teter and Bob Buckler, Julie and Scott Stockert, Kay and Roger Aitchison, Dana Silkensen, Christine and Mark Piquette, Marcie and Rob Decker, Susan and Jeff Lutz, Renee and Chris Price, Noelle and Mike Abarelli, and Jabe Hickey and Eve Canfield: I adore you all.

Lisa Jones and Peter Williams, you made Colorado home.

Molly Gordon, Mark Silver, Eric Klein, and Michael Bungay Stanier, you make me smarter, braver, and up my skill at sick silly jokes immeasurably. You hauled me out of the depths so many times. I love you.

To my incredibly generous and perceptive beta readers, Anne Walsh, Tara Mohr, and Hiro Boga, you made this book a hundred times better.

Special thanks to book coach Jennie Nash who freed me from the death grip of my memoir and helped me get this book off the ground with her clarifying questions and can-do spirit. Without you, I might still be trying to burn down the barn and find the moon.

A hearty hug to Janet Goldstein for the question "What's fresh for you now?" and for your honesty about that *other* book. Our conversation helped me see what I'd been writing about all along.

Thank you, Marianne Elliott, for reading an earlier draft and for your constant goodness in my world. Thank you, Natalie Serber, Anna Guest-Jelley, and Susan Piver for writer pep talks, friendship, and subtitle help. Gratitude to Ann Cheng, Billie Taylor, Mary Davies, Elizabeth Turner, Anna Bunting, Maggie Davis, and Kim Schiffer for all the times you reminded me I belong.

To Tressa, Berit, Becky, Ashlee, Rachel, and Jay, you have made so much of what went into this book possible, by taking such good care of my students and clients and by helping me believe my ideas can become reality. I am able to be so much more because of your kindness and care and the fact you catch my mistakes.

Melani Dizon, you consistently blow me away with your ideas, energy, and care. Many thanks for what you brought to my business, which laid the foundation for this work.

Sue and Joel Sorem, I am so lucky to have you as my bonus mom and dad.

Michele, you stepped up with such courage and love to take care of mom. Thank you for how much you loved mom and for the freedom you gave me to write this book.

Aidan, thank you for letting me be your bonus mom. You are the kind of man the world needs more of. I am so lucky to have you in my life.

Lillian, I'll always love you more, and aren't I the luckiest person in the world to get to? Thank you for forgiving me all my mistakes, especially during *those* years. With your forgiveness, I made a new life.

Bobby, you made this story possible. When I said to you, "I can really have this, can't I?" and you said, "You can, baby, of course, you can," you showed me it's okay to be happy. We *were* in each other all along. I will love you forever and longer if I can.

And to you, my reader, please believe me when I say if I can find my way to a "most human" life, a life that makes me tear up in wonder, you can too. There is nothing you lack, nothing that has to be fixed first, nothing that forever blocks you from more. I promise.

Notes

A FULL LIST OF books, resources, and other useful material is available at jenniferlouden.com/whybother, kept up to date along with new recommended resources.

Chapter 5: Leave Behind

"We live in an unjust world"

For statistics and sources about income inequality, visit inequality.org/facts/income-inequality/. For information about Black American women's earnings compared to white men, go to equalpaytoday.org/black-womens-equal-pay-day-2019 and read the report at aauw.org/research/the-simple-truth-about-the-gender-pay-gap/.

Chapter 6: Ease In

"The cost of not being able to express our anger is enormous"

Deborah Cox, Karin H. Bruckner, and Sally D. Stabb, *The Anger Advantage: The Surprising Benefits of Anger and How It Can Change a Woman's Life* (Broadway Books, 2003), pages 82 and 126.

Benjamin P. Chapman, Kevin Fiscella, Ichiro Kawachi, Paul Duberstein, and Peter Muennig, "Emotion Suppression and Mortality Risk over a 12-Year Follow-up," *Journal of Psychosomatic Research* 75(4), 2013, pages 381–385. DOI: 10.1016/j.jpsychores.2013.07.014.

"Research shows that African American girls maintain higher self-esteem than boys through high school"

Soraya Chemaly, *Rage Becomes Her: The Power of Women's Anger* (Atria Books, 2018), page 24.

Jeanne Saunders, Larry Davis, Trina Williams, and James Herbert Williams, "Gender Differences in Self-Perceptions and Academic Outcomes," *Journal of Youth and Adolescence* 33(1), February 2004, pages 81–90. DOI: 10.1023/A:1027390531768.

Chapter 9: Become by Doing

"I don't think that loving yourself is a choice"

Lizzo, "Self-Care Has to Be Rooted in Self-Preservation, Not Just Mimosas and Spa Cays," NBC Think, April 19, 2019. nbcnews.com/think/opinion/self-care-has-be-rooted-self-preservation-not-just-mimosas-ncna993661.

Also of Interest

Various studies have shown cynical people to have overall poorer health, higher rates of mortality, and increased likelihood of dementia; see Dr. Hilary Tindle's *Up: How Positive Outlook Can Transform Our Health and Aging* (Avery/Penguin, 2013), which cites several studies on pages 6 and 9.

People with high levels of cynical distrust may be more likely to develop dementia, according to the following studies: Elisa Neuvonen, Minna Rusanen, Alina Solomon, et al., "Late-Life Cynical Distrust, Risk of Incident Dementia, and Mortality in a Population-Based Cohort," *Neurology* 82(24), 2014. DOI: 10.1212/WNL.0000000000000528.

Jane Cauley, Stephen Smagula, Kathleen Hovey, et al., "Optimism, Cynical Hostility, Falls, and Fractures: The Women's Health Initiative Observational Study (WHIOS)," *Journal of Bone and Mineral Research* 32(2), August 27, 2016. DOI: 10.1002/jbmr.2984.

Ana Progovac, Julie Donohue, Karen Matthews, et al., "Optimism Predicts Sustained Vigorous Physical Activity in Postmenopausal Women," *Preventive Medicine Reports* 8, December 2017, pages 286–293. DOI: 10.1016/j.pmedr.2017.10.008.

About the Author

———

J ENNIFER LOUDEN wanted to be Harriet the Spy when she was eight, an enlightened master when she was twelve, and a brilliant comedy writer when she was twenty-two. She penned her bestseller, *The Woman's Comfort Book*, after her first *why bother* time. She's the author of five additional books including *The Woman's Retreat Book* and *The Life Organizer*. She has inspired millions of women through her books, her retreats and workshops, and her blog, but probably not her fashion sense and certainly not her cooking.

———

Has this book helped you get your bother on?

I'd appreciate if you left a review online with your preferred retailer. Reviews help readers find my book, which will spread the word about the importance of bothering again. Thank you.

Want to buy multiple copies of *Why Bother?* for your writers' group, team, class, or company? Wonderful. I can help. I can also help you customize *Why Bother?* for your organization and you can hire me to bring the ideas in *Why Bother?* alive through my interactive workshops and keynotes.

Contact my team at jen@jenniferlouden.com for more information.